IN THE DRIVING SEAT

IN THE DRIVING SEAT

A Guide to the Grand Prix Circuits

Nigel Mansell

and Derick Allsop

Stanley Paul

London Sydney Auckland Johannesburg

Stanley Paul and Co. Ltd

An imprint of Century Hutchinson Ltd

Brookmount House, 62–65 Chandos Place,
Covent Garden, London WC2N 4NW

Century Hutchinson Australia (Pty) Ltd
88–91 Albion Street, Surry Hills, NSW 2010

Century Hutchinson New Zealand Limited
191 Archers Road, PO Box 40–086, Glenfield, Auckland 10

Century Hutchinson South Africa (Pty) Ltd
PO Box 337, Bergvlei 2012, South Africa

First published in 1989

Set in Century Old Style and News Gothic by
🅰 Tek Art Ltd, Croydon, Surrey

Printed and bound by
Butler and Tanner Ltd, Frome, Somerset

Cataloguing in Publication Data
Mansell, Nigel
    In the driving Seat: the Grand Prix Circuits
    1. Race tracks. Racing cars Racing
    I. Title   II. Allsop, Derick
    796.7'2'068

ISBN 0 09 173818 0

Contents

We wish to thank the many for their time and assistance in the construction of this guide-book. Chief among those to whom we are indebted are: Sue Allsop, Ann Bradshaw, Brands Hatch Circuit, Bob Constanduros, Jardine PR, Sue Membery, Silverstone Circuit, and Stuart Sykes.

Foreword

Co-authors Nigel Mansell and Derick Allsop. Each contributes his own opinions and observations to this book. Derick goes first and the text is separated by broad rules. Derick Allsop, born in Chesterfield, Derbyshire, has covered Grand Prix motor racing for the Daily Mail *since 1981*

Even for the vast majority of racing drivers, the prospect of sitting behind the wheel of a Grand Prix car is no more than a dream. The Formula One World Championship is the pinnacle of a sport which lures thousands of enthusiasts to tracks of diverse standard and nature all round the globe. Only twenty-six drivers qualify for the supreme privilege and challenge of a title race.

For those who can never aspire to such heights – and those who would never wish to anyway – Nigel Mansell offers the opportunity to share his view of Grand Prix racing. He gives a graphic cockpit guide to the Championship circuits, highlighting their particular features and requirements. He details the speeds, the gears and the lines to be taken along the annual intercontinental trek.

Formula One is ever-changing, ever-advancing. Indeed Mansell's new team, Ferrari, have pioneered work on a seven-speed, semi-automatic gearbox. But for most that is a distant development. The norm remains the six-speed gearbox, and Nigel's analyses are based on laps in a conventional car. His insight is complemented by historical and statistical information about the circuits in an attempt to provide a complete companion for the Grand Prix voyeur.

Derick Allsop
February, 1989

INTRODUCTION

Around the globe, from Brazil to Britain, Mexico to Monaco, and America to Australia, the Grand Prix marathon winds its annual course of drama, spectacle and emotion. Sixteen circuits – no two of them alike – will test the quality and resilience of man and machine to determine the ultimate prize in motor racing, the Formula One World Championship.

OUR Championship is the highest peak of the sport, the greatest challenge for a racing driver. To justify that stature it has to be tough in terms of the opposition and the circuits. The top drivers are attracted to Formula One, and the tracks provide the varied conditions and demands to stretch them to the limit.

CART racing in North America is a fantastic series and I certainly would not want to knock it, but it is inevitably limited because it exists on one continent. The Formula One World Championship is precisely what it says. It covers the world and it is Number One.

Formula One is multi-national in terms of drivers and venues. Just as the drivers vary in character and dimension, so too do the circuits. We start in Brazil, we cross over to Europe for a couple of races, then it's Mexico and North America. We return for the main chunk of the European season before heading for Japan and the finale in Australia. It's a hectic, tiring, but exciting journey. No other series can compare with it.

The circuits are as individual as the countries in which they are situated. They reflect the different histories, cultures and languages. That all adds to the appeal of the Championship. FISA are now doing a fantastic job around the world, standardizing circuit safety requirements. But that hasn't meant changing circuits to the extent where they become the same. That would be boring not only for the spectators but also for the drivers.

New tracks have been built into the season alongside the traditional, established circuits and that is good. The sport should be moving all the time, looking to different countries and audiences. In 1986 we went behind the Iron Curtain, to Hungary, and no doubt there are more new venues to come.

I broadly categorize circuits in terms of speed: fast, medium and slow. Some circuits nudge towards another category, but generally they will fall into one of those three slots. Monaco, and Hungary are all slow-speed circuits, but while Monaco is very slow, Hungary is close to being medium speed. They are all very demanding, hard work-rate circuits.

Above: *Eyes on the track*

Right:
Monaco . . . slowest of the Grand Prix circuits

The next one very close to this category is Jerez, in Spain, which has lots of corners. Jerez and the Hungaroring, Budapest, gave my 1988 car, the normally aspirated Canon Williams Judd, rare opportunities to compete against the turbos. Now, of course, there are no turbos so hopefully there will be a lot more close racing.

The medium-speed circuits, which vary greatly and account for about half the Grand Prix venues, include places like Rio, Montreal, Estoril and probably Adelaide. Although Adelaide is, like Monaco, a street circuit, it has a long straight and is much more like a true racetrack.

Up in the high-speed category you have Silverstone, Hockenheim, Spa and Monza. All have very long straights, where speeds can top 200 m.p.h. Silverstone, home of the British Grand Prix until 1990, is the fastest of all, with *average* speeds of well over 150 m.p.h. Its great rival for the title of 'Fastest Track' was the Osterreichring, at Zeltweg, Austria, but that is no longer on the calendar.

Silverstone . . . the fastest

What we have is a great mix of circuits, and they present the drivers with a range of genuine challenges. We don't have American-style oval circuits, and I can't really comment on them because I've never actually driven on one. But I have spoken to many drivers who have and they say you have to adopt a different driving style. To a certain extent you have to de-tune. You're flat out and completing a lap in thirty seconds or less in some cases.

Indianapolis is the great circuit and the 500 is such a very special event, but CART racing now takes in a lot of road-race circuits. Rick Mears, a master of ovals, has said he struggled for a while to adapt when he had to switch to more road tracks. He had to learn a whole new technique. Being such a good driver, he was able to do that and he is now outstanding on both types of circuit. It just proves, however, that you can't go straight from oval to road and, equally, I don't think you could switch straight from road to oval and be at your best.

Over the years our tracks have been revised and modified as FISA have met the demands for improved safety standards, but I don't think that has taken away their individuality. In essence, they are the same tracks. Their general structure and features haven't changed and that is good. You know what to expect, and there are some places you love going back to.

Equally, there are one or two circuits that I don't like so much and don't really look forward to. But if you dwell on the negative you become unprofessional and put up a barrier for yourself. I keep my feelings about these circuits to myself because I have to go to every race venue with a positive view. That's the only way you can hope to be professional about the job and carry it through to the best of your ability. You know you don't like this particular place or corner, and it isn't a problem admitting it to yourself. But you mustn't let the others know your feelings because that is revealing a weakness that they may be able to exploit.

I'm not alone in having my likes and dislikes. Every driver has his favourite circuits and others where he says, 'Oh no, here we go.' The

trick is to apply yourself wherever you are. That, too, is part of the challenge of Formula One. You have to adapt to the different tracks, time zones, climates, foods and nationalities. It is, in every sense, the *true* World Championship.

A fairly recent trend has been to contain speeds through the introduction of chicanes. This is a relatively simple and cheap way of modifying a circuit, forcing the cars to slow into a tight, twisting corner or section put in to slow an existing corner or break up a long fast straight. Hockenheim and Monza are examples of where this has been done. At Spa they have the distinctive 'Bus Stop' chicane.

I accept the purpose and merit of chicanes in general and I welcome some of them. Others I don't welcome so readily. I don't particularly like those where you just bounce off the kerbs. Monza is a place I love because of its very special atmosphere, its history, its partisan crowd. You can get 250,000 people there over a race weekend. That's fantastic support. But down on the track you have to deal with those chicanes, and that isn't so fantastic. You face a dreadful dilemma because if you want a fast lap you have to go over the kerbs. All that bouncing around does the driver and often the car no good. The kerbs are, unfortunately, part of the Monza package now and you have to put up with them.

Clearly it makes more sense to change the cars rather than keep rebuilding the circuits. Technology moves on at such a pace that circuits would soon become obsolete if the regulations weren't constantly reviewed and amended. Some corners can become very, very dangerous with the download of the modern cars. Cornering speeds have become incredible. Now the turbos have gone, but you can be sure that the speeds will increase again with the inevitable investment and development that goes into Formula One. So much is at stake.

Spa's distinctive 'Bus Stop' chicane

You can change the tracks only so much, and it is not just a matter of expense. You can make a corner wider and safer to the point where the driver no longer finds it the great challenge it once was. Also the spectators find themselves pushed further and further away from the action to the point where it loses its appeal for them.

Jerez has been designed with the spectators' as well as the drivers' safety in mind. As yet we do not, unfortunately, have big crowds there, but those who do turn up for the Grand Prix have excellent viewing facilities. In fact, I'm generally impressed with the new circuits. I cannot overemphasize the importance of the safety measures: good run-off areas and barriers; good medical organization. Yet still the circuits are challenging and the stands give the public splendid views of the best of the action.

I personally don't have a particular preference for fast circuits or slow circuits. I judge them individually in terms of the challenge and the atmosphere. Monaco has long been one of my favourite tracks. It is a narrow, twisting, street circuit, and, I believe, the greatest challenge of all. You have to be precise. Even the slightest error can put you out of the race. Look what happened to Ayrton Senna in 1988. He was on his way to victory but got slightly off line and hit the barrier. Anywhere else he would probably have got away with it, but he was unlucky, this was Monaco. It is so much more than a race. It is a very, very special event and I always get a charge from the place.

Monaco is the slowest circuit, but I also get a great kick out of Silverstone, which is the quickest. Monaco is all up and down,

Silverstone is flat. Your home circuit naturally means something different, yet I find those fast corners and straights truly exhilarating. There are plenty of overtaking opportunities, so it's real, high-speed *racing*.

Concentration is essential on the track. When you're going through the corners you are working anyway, so there's no problem. On the straight your mind may wander a bit, but only in a positive way. You may say, 'this is a long race' or 'it's going well, I just hope everything is holding together'.

If I have a few seconds to spare, I go through a bit of a routine. 'How's the gearbox feeling? Not bad. Brakes, engine, clutch, steering, tyres, aerodynamics, track conditions?' If the track is breaking up you programme your mind to say 'a couple of corners are dangerous, leave a little margin because if you slip a bit wide you're in the wall.'

A typical example of this problem was Detroit. Just think how many drivers – including myself – have gone into the wall there. Turn Three and the last turn have claimed many, many cars over the years and it's not necessarily because the drivers have made mistakes. It's because the track conditions have deteriorated so much.

Therefore you have to be prepared to allow that inch, even that half an inch, because it can make all the difference. An error by even that small amount can be costly. You're gone. So you go through all these things very quickly in your mind, feel and weigh them up, and then get back on with the job.

These days we have radio contact with our teams, but that is no substitute for the old pitboards. The radio is a useful aid, but it is still secondary to the pitboard. The radio is all right for the driver to use one way, but if an engineer chooses a bad moment to try to speak to the driver he could actually cause an accident. You take some corners at 160 m.p.h. or more and have to judge distances to the half inch, therefore any distraction could make you miss the apex and crash. The radio is a piece of equipment that should always be taken seriously.

In the early days, long before radios and such high cornering speeds, there were only seven or eight races to the season. However, partly due to increased demand and improved travel facilities, the number has now reached sixteen. There is even talk of still more races, but you have to remember that the working year also includes a lot of testing; to add more races would be too much of a burden for drivers and mechanics alike. The last thing you want is overstrained teams with tired drivers and personnel. Sixteen is just about the optimum figure.

As a new season approaches I always feel eager anticipation. Yes, as I've said, there are a couple of places I don't relish so much, but there are far more that I enjoy. Anywhere with a good golf course is one to look forward to: like Monaco, Estoril and the North American races. It's also nice to get some sunshine. But the real appeal is still the racing, and we have the Formula One circuits to captivate any racer.

1 BRAZIL

Circuit: *Jacarepagua*

Rio de Janeiro: beautiful and bizarre, vibrant and violent. Few other cities in the world − if, indeed, any − are cradled in such natural splendour. This home for eight million people is bordered by dazzling beaches and black and green mountains.

The travelling community of Formula One has made Rio its first camp of the season. Some of the more affluent teams will have been here already for testing. Some of the not so affluent will have had to make do with humbler preparations. Rio does not discriminate. It divides the classes among locals and visitors alike.

The spirit of the Carnival never dissipates. The hot sun, the ready Carioca smile, the brown buttocks, the Copacabana joggers and the endless *churrascarias* (barbecue houses) bring to life all the fantasies of a Brazilian holiday. But reality in Rio also encompasses the less palatable. Beneath the giant figure of Christ the Redeemer, survival is a doubtful blessing for those that live in the Favelas, the shanties.

Below left: *Jacarepagua . . . the track that rose from the marshes*

Below right: *The clouds roll off the mountains, the cars roll off the grid*

One member of the Formula One community virtually adopted a young boy for the duration of his visit. The following year the boy was there again, his beaming if scruffy face registering approval of any little treat. The man from Formula One decided it was time to smarten up his little friend, took him to a store and dressed him from head to toe. An ugly duckling no more, he preened himself in front of his chums.

Next day the man from a distant land went looking for the kid again and, to his horror, saw him back in his tatty togs. 'Where are your new clothes,' asked the man. The boy replied by rubbing together his thumb and forefinger. Man may not live on bread alone, but Rio boy finds a little helps.

By day the beaches are alive with gorgeous girls and the brilliant fledgling footballers. By night they are the hunting ground for muggers. Some years ago a Grand Prix team official was stabbed. More recently the British driver Jonathan Palmer had his thigh slashed by a youth

armed with a broken bottle. Former driver Innes Ireland and his lady, brandishing her high-heeled shoe, fought off a gang intent on relieving them of all their valuables.

Even the Atlantic Ocean can be dangerous. In 1981 Peter Collins — then a Lotus official, now Benetton team boss — was saved from drowning by Nigel Mansell. These days drivers and officials tend to stick to their hotels and pools, on the circuit side of the city.

The Jacarepagua circuit is built on reclaimed marshland, about eighteen miles west of the other action. It is flat and not the most inspiring of tracks, but the backdrop of mountains and the colourful, buzzing open stands create a dramatic sporting arena. The crowd sit for hours in the unrelenting sun. As the temperature rises to 100 degrees and beyond, the fire brigade are called in to apply a cooling spray. The shower is gratefully received by the punters.

Above: *The Zakspeed moves over, the Williams moves on*

Left: *Cooling off period for the Brazilian fans*

Rio's weather can, however, be erratic. Storms are as violent as the muggers. In 1988 hospitality units were flattened and one man narrowly escaped death when a massive advertising hoarding crashed down.

Jacarepagua first staged the Brazilian Grand Prix in 1978 and took the race on a permanent basis from the much-acclaimed Interlagos circuit of Sao Paolo in 1981, Nigel Mansell's first full season in Formula One. In 1983 Jacarepagua opened the Championship, and has had the honour ever since. Financial problems — a familiar feature of Brazilian life — have constantly threatened the race. The 1989 event was no exception after the city declared itself bankrupt and the circuit was put up for sale.

In its relatively short Grand Prix life, Jacarepagua has had its share of drama and controversy. In 1982 Brazilian Nelson Piquet finished first, with Keke Rosberg second. But both were disqualified and Alain Prost was declared the winner. Piquet, close to collapse on the podium, had his revenge victory the following year, though there was no change of fortune for Rosberg. The defending champion tried to jump clear of a flash fire as fuel was pumped into his tank during a pit stop. He was pushed back into his car and onto the track to finish behind Piquet again. But the stewards disqualified him for that push start.

Ayrton Senna was disqualified in 1988 for changing cars after the green flag. That race was won by Alain Prost, his fifth success here in seven years. Nigel Mansell had only five points from eight races until his glorious debut victory for Ferrari in 1989.

W<small>E</small> come out of the European winter to start the season thousands of miles away, in a hot, incredibly humid climate. It's wise, therefore, to get there a couple of days before the first practice to acclimatize. I did cut it rather fine in 1987 when our plane broke down, though I still managed to get pole.

It's also wise to have all your senses working in Rio. It can be the most romantic place, yet it can also be the most dangerous.

As a workplace it leaves a lot to be desired. The drivers and team officials can at least escape into air-conditioned cabins between the sessions, but for the mechanics it can be horrendous. At night – and they often work well into the night – they are eaten alive by mosquitoes and various other creatures. People are constantly passing out. I haven't known a year when someone hasn't been admitted to hospital.

The Brazilian Grand Prix is a demanding race, both by the nature of the place and because it is the first race of the season. Although we've been testing, there's no substitute for racing. If mistakes are going to be made they are probably going to be made at the first race.

The circuit is medium to high speed. It has a variety of corners, including some high-speed ones, so you're coping with a lot of G-force.

Mansell chases the McLaren into the first corner

It's particularly hard here because it is an exception to the general rule – it's an anti-clockwise circuit. What neck muscles you built up in the previous year are for a clockwise circuit!

Rio is uncompromising with a lot of its corners. You make a bit of an error, get just a little off line and you can be into the dusty parts and off the circuit. It's also, in parts, extremely bumpy. That can take its toll on both the driver and the car. When you hit these bumps, throwing up sparks from under the car, you are getting eighteen to twenty G-loading shock waves through the car and through your body. Reliability is vital anywhere, but here more so than at many circuits.

Another important factor for driver and engine is the heat. It can drain you, as many drivers have discovered. You must take in as much fluid as you can. With Williams we had temperature problems. You must get the radiator sizes right. With so much waste paper and rubbish blowing about the radiator ducts easily get blocked. If your engine overheats your race is run.

Rio is not too bad on brakes, but the surface is very abrasive and hard on the tyres. As you go through the practice sessions more and more rubber is put down, so that by race day it may not be so serious a problem. There can, though, be plenty of other problems to contend

. . . and this time the Ferrari

with. A lot of cars fail to finish and a lot of drivers have miserable records here.

I think that's a reflection of the fact that it's the first race of the season, in a hot climate. The drivers are probably not at their best and there are a number of things still not right with the car. But the atmosphere at the race is good. The crowd are, not surprisingly, overenthusiastic for their own, but they are reasonably fair. You certainly get a buzz from the place. And I had an unbelievable start with Ferrari when I won in 1989.

Lap of Jacarepagua

Across the start and finish line you're going up from fifth gear to sixth, clearing the length of the pits, and then going down to fourth as you come into the first right-hander. You don't want to lose time here. You need to get it right and get through the corner as quickly as possible, changing out of the exit in fifth gear, probably travelling at 140 to 150 m.p.h.

Staying in fifth, it's a quick, short straight to Pace corner, the first left-hander. You're braking and changing down to fourth, possibly third, depending on your ratios, accelerating round here at about 120 m.p.h. Coming clear of Pace you take fifth gear, and hold it in fifth flat out through the Suspiro Corner.

This is a very dangerous left-hander. You're having to contend with opposite camber on the exit. You get into it and think it's fine, no problem, but then halfway across the track it falls away to the outside of the circuit and, unless you're careful, you're spinning the car. I've had a few moments here, though fortunately not any nasty ones.

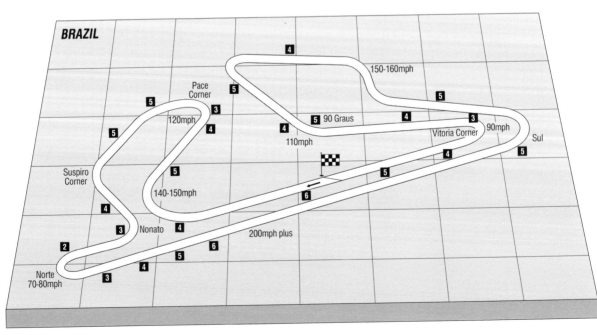

Coming through and clear of Suspiro, you change down to fourth, sometimes third, depending on how slippery it is, for the right-hander Nonato. Accelerate up to the hairpin, which is Norte, changing down to second. This is one of the very bumpy bits. You've got to hug the inside line at about 70 to 80 m.p.h. It's easy to understeer off the circuit here.

Out of Norte, up through the gears: to third, fourth, fifth, sixth, down the main straight as quick as your engine will take you, upwards of 200 m.p.h. Good overtaking opportunity towards Sul. Just a little dab on the brakes, down to fifth gear and then flat out.

At this sweeping left-hander you have four to four-and-a-half lateral G-force. It's quick. Get it wrong and you're looking at a big accident. There's only one line and a bump going in. Then it's a quick flick right, which again I take in fifth, for the first of a sequence of three corners.

You have to be precise from the first. If you get the first one right, the other two will flow. Get the first one wrong, and you're struggling with the other two. After the right, it's an immediate flick left. Take these two corners at 150 to 160 m.p.h.

Down to fourth for the tight left-hander. Incredible G-loading because you have positive camber on your side. That is to say the track slopes from the outside to the inside of the corner, which gives you the positive G as well as the lateral G. The car, of course, goes round the corner quicker than it would if the track was flat. It puts a lot of strain on your neck, especially, and on your arms.

Accelerating up to fifth gear down to the 90 Graus Corner, a left-hander. Down to third or fourth depending on the gear ratios. Speed about 100 m.p.h. Accelerating through the corner, adverse camber coming out, almost hitting the kerb, then up to fifth gear for the final hairpin, the Vitoria Corner.

Again down to third gear. It's a little faster than Norte Corner, probably approaching 90 m.p.h. Got to hug the inside here. Not a lot of grip to help you. Bit of understeer, bit of oversteer. It's a 180-degree corner that seems to go on forever. Out of the corner at last, accelerating on to the start and finish straight, up to fourth, fifth and going for sixth as you cross the line to complete the lap.

Jacarepagua Fact file

Circuit length: 3·126 miles, 5·031 km.
Race distance: 61 laps (190·693 miles, 306·891 km.)
Qualifying lap record: Ayrton Senna (McLaren Honda) 1m. 25·302s., in 1989
Race lap record: Riccardo Patrese (Williams Renault) 1m. 32·507s. at 121·583 m.p.h., in 1989

Winners: 1978, Carlos Reutemann (Ferrari); 1981, Carlos Reutemann (Williams Ford); 1982, Alain Prost (Renault); 1983, Nelson Piquet (Brabham BMW); 1984, Alain Prost (McLaren TAG); 1985, Alain Prost (McLaren TAG); 1986, Nelson Piquet (Williams Honda); 1987, Alain Prost (McLaren TAG); 1988, Alain Prost (McLaren Honda); 1989, Nigel Mansell (Ferrari)

Nigel Mansell: 1981, 11th (Lotus Ford); 1982, 3rd (Lotus Ford); 1983, 12th (Lotus Ford); 1984, accident (Lotus Renault); 1985, retired (Williams Honda); 1986, accident (Williams Honda); 1987, 6th (Williams Honda); 1988, retired (Williams Judd); 1989, 1st (Ferrari)

2 SAN MARINO

Circuit: Imola *(Autodromo Enzo and Dino Ferrari)*

Italian spring — gentle sunshine, occasional rain — welcomes Formula One to Europe. The hospitality in Romagna is good. The pasta is exceptional, the wine liberally dispensed and gratefully received.

The Grand Prix is attributed to San Marino, a tiny republic perched high on a rock just inland from the bustling holiday resort of Rimini. The fact is, of course, that the title is convenient. In reality it simply means Italy has a second race. Italians long argued that France had, in essence, two Grands Prix, its own and Monaco's. The retort that the Monaco Grand Prix is actually held *in* Monaco while Imola is almost fifty miles from San Marino is dismissed as an irrelevance.

All the arguments are in the past, anyway. Imola, which staged the 1980 Italian Grand Prix, has hosted the San Marino Grand Prix ever since 1981 and the event has become one of the most popular on the calendar.

Imola, twenty miles southeast of Bologna, where the magnificent Apennines tumble towards sea level, is a Roman town, inevitably slightly faded and worn, but none the less endearing for that. It has a calm, dignified air; a setting perhaps more suited to cultural pursuits than motorised combat.

The circuit is on the edge of the town, a road that climbs and dips, sweeps and wiggles but never quite straightens. It is the closest major track to Ferrari headquarters at Maranello and was named after Enzo

Above: *Imola . . . Roman town, motorized combat*

Left: *The* tifosi *follow Mansell's progress, in 1988*

Right: *. . . and take their places wherever they can*

Above left: *Didier Pironi leads Gilles Villeneuve through the last chicane*

Above right: *. . . and across the line in 1982*

Ferrari's son Dino, who died of muscular dystrophy in 1956 at the age of twenty-four.

This may be Ferrari country, but the atmosphere is never quite so hostile and frenzied as at Monza. The Ferrari fans are there all right. In their scores of thousands. They pack the huge banks that form natural galleries; they fill the balconies of houses overlooking the track; they erect scaffolding or scale the perimeter fencing. All of them waving Prancing Horse flags. They tend, however, to be more laid back than the Monza *tifosi*.

Not that they contained their emotions in 1982 when Ferrari pair Gilles Villeneuve and Didier Pironi turned the race into a domestic squabble. Villeneuve, as No. 1 driver, anticipated no resistance from his partner and tried to contain the pace of the contest every time he took the lead. But fired up Pironi refused to yield and took the flag, much to the Canadian's anger.

Villeneuve was fatally injured in practice for the next race, in Belgium. Pironi was distraught and the Italian public, who virtually beatified their beloved Villeneuve, would not ease the Frenchman's sense of guilt. Later that season Pironi was badly injured when he seemed destined for the Championship. He never raced in Formula One again. The final twist to this sad tale came in 1987, when Pironi was killed in a powerboat accident.

The Imola fans were wholly unsympathetic when, in 1983, a fellow countryman, Riccardo Patrese, crashed off the track. Nothing personal, it was just that Patrese drove a Brabham and his misfortune let in Frenchman Patrick Tambay – who drove a Ferrari. The roar of approval was for the car.

For 1989 the Ferrari fans welcomed a new man to support. Nigel Mansell's committed, charging style appeals to the Italians, and at the

wheel of the scarlet Ferrari he knew he would be guaranteed a phenomenal reception. Success would assure him hero-worship on a scale he had never previously experienced.

A young Mansell, then the third Lotus driver, was unable to qualify for the Italian Grand Prix here in 1980. He didn't enter in 1981, when the San Marino Grand Prix was launched, or in 1982, the year of the FOCA boycott over their conflict with FISA. He finally raced here in 1983, and was classified twelfth. In 1984 he retired and in 1985, with Williams, managed fifth place.

That 1985 San Marino Grand Prix was one of the most extraordinary races in the history of Formula One. Imola is a thirsty track, and one by one the queue of contenders for victory staggered to a halt as their tanks ran dry with the flag still tantalizingly beyond reach. Eventually Alain Prost made it to the line – only to be disqualified because his car was underweight. The verdict ultimately went to Nigel's former Lotus team-mate, Elio de Angelis.

After another enforced retirement in 1986, Mansell's luck turned in 1987. He stayed the course and claimed victory. In 1988 and in 1989 he produced typically bold performances, only for his equipment to fail again.

Right: *Crowd pleaser . . . Patrick Tambay steers the Ferrari to victory in 1983*

I haven't always had the best of breaks at Imola, and I suppose my misfortune in 1988 sums up a lot of my races here. But on the positive side I have been a winner, and I was looking for a possible third place while I was running in 1988. Now, of course, the race holds a particular significance for me. And I was given a phenomenal reception when I turned up for the 1989 San Marino Grand Prix. It seemed that all Italy was still celebrating our win in Brazil a month earlier.

As a Ferrari driver racing in Italy is now very special for me. I've always had good support from the Italian fans, but now it is something else. We all know what Ferrari means to Italians. We've all seen the scenes at Imola and Monza, and heard them roar on their red cars. But actually to be in one of those cars and have all that support behind me is an incredible experience.

Apart from the fact that this is the home of Ferrari, it's good to be at a European circuit, with all the advantages in terms of travel, time zones and facilities. You get into a routine with European races. Fly in on the Thursday, go to the track, chat to the team, run over the plans for the weekend. Friday and Saturday mornings we have one-and-a-half-hour's free practice, in the afternoons the one-hour qualifying sessions. In the evenings we may have sponsors' engagements, otherwise just a quiet meal. Sunday morning there's a half-hour warm-up, which is the final practice. The race is Sunday afternoon, usually a 2.30 start in Europe, then afterwards, it's straight back home.

After the heat and all the other possible problems of Rio, Imola is well appreciated. A feature of European races is the paddock, which is really like a little village. The teams have motorhomes with catering and hospitality facilities for personnel, sponsors and guests. You can pop next door for a chat and, like any village, there's lots of gossip.

The pit complex at Imola is very good. The garages are large enough to enable the teams to get in their equipment and work properly. Again, this is an area where FISA are rightly demanding high standards. Similarly with Press facilities. At Imola the Press centre, fax and phone rooms are above the pits. In the same block there are also hospitality suites, and a restaurant where the pasta is as good as you would hope.

This again, is an anti-clockwise circuit, and very difficult in that you can never set up the car perfectly for every part of it. You have to find a delicate balance. It's a compromise circuit. You have a long, long straight – in fact more a curve than a straight – but then a lot of tight corners, which make it more of a fast-medium than truly fast circuit.

It's an interesting and challenging circuit. It's very varied in terms of corners and the gradients. Get the aerodynamics right for the whole circuit and you'd win it every time. But it's very satisfying when you know you've got it as right as you're ever going to get it, and you've put in a clean, quick lap.

*Chequered flag for Nigel
Mansell in 1987*

Lap of Imola

Coming to the start and finish line you're changing up from fourth to fifth, and then sixth virtually as you cross the line. You're now heading towards this long sweep of a left-hander, the Tamburello, which you take flat out in sixth. At this point you're probably up to 160 to 170 m.p.h. already, and you've still got half the straight to go. Along this stretch, the Villeneuve Straight, you're up to 200 m.p.h., but even here there's a little kink in the road.

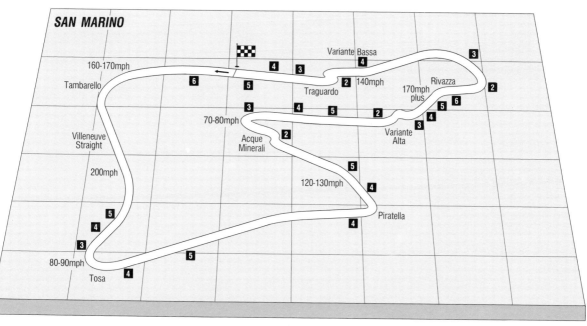

Ahead now is Tosa, a tight left-hander. You're braking hard, very hard. Down through the gears, sixth to third very quickly. There's a good run-off area here so you don't have to worry too much if your brakes fail! It can be a little uncomfortable if you do go off, though. Brakes are always a major concern at this circuit.

Nigel exits the top chicane, 1988

You're round Tosa in third, probably doing 80 to 90 m.p.h. Exit, then up to fourth and fifth, quickly climbing the hill. It was all this hard braking and accelerating that caused the turbos so many fuel consumption problems. Holding fifth over the brow, and braking down into fourth for the left-hand Piratella corner. Flat out in fourth, 120 to 130 m.p.h., and down the hill in fifth towards Acqua Minerali.

Here we are into a sequence of corners, starting with a very tight chicane. Again, you're braking hard, down from fifth to second. It's a

flick right, flick left. You have to get through here smoothly, without hitting the kerbs, because they are nine inches or more in height. Go over them and you can destroy your car.

Accelerating, third gear. Next right-hander. Very quick, very slippery at times. Must get it right. If you got the first part of the sequence right you should flow. If not, you could have a struggle on your hands. You'd be fighting to get back. Hopefully you've got it right, and taken those second- and third-gear corners at 70 to 80 m.p.h.

Now it's uphill again. Fourth and fifth, before braking to take the Variante Alta chicane in second. Right, left, got to be perfect. Bit of wheel-spin coming out. Up through the gears, third, fourth, fifth, sixth. You're onto another curved stretch, going under the bridge and downhill to the Rivazza, flat out at 170-plus m.p.h.

Here you're approaching a hairpin and braking incredibly hard. It's a left-hander, adverse camber, and your brakes have to be right. Get a locking wheel at this point and you can miss the corner. Take it in second. It's very slow. Then up to third for the second part of the left-hander, which is much quicker.

Now you're onto a short straight to come back into the stadium at Variante Bassa. Up to fourth and, if the car is perfect, even fifth, and flat out. This is a frightening corner because it's a switchback. It's right and then left and, as you're going through at 140 m.p.h., you're pushed from one side of the cockpit to the other. This is quite a spectacular section of the circuit, and the spectators up on the hill get a fabulous view of the cars making their way towards the final chicane.

Braking down hard for this chicane, which is the Traguardo. Second gear. Got to be careful not to overshoot or you're into the pits. The entrance to the pits is on the right-hand side of this corner. One line, so get it right. There are kerbs on the inside and outside. Bounce over them and you throw away half a second or a second. As you are in the slide coming out of the corner, change to third and accelerate all the way up to the start/finish line. It's a hard-going circuit, but get it right and it's very rewarding.

Imola Fact file

Circuit length: 3·132 miles, 5·040 km.
Race distance: 60 laps (187·92 miles, 302·40 km.)
Qualifying lap record: Ayrton Senna (Lotus Renault) 1m. 25·050s., in 1986
Race lap record: Alain Prost (McLaren Honda) 1m. 26·795s. at 129·899 m.p.h., in 1989

Winners: Italian Grand Prix – 1980, Nelson Piquet (Brabham Ford). San Marino Grand Prix – 1981, Nelson Piquet (Brabham Ford); 1982, Didier Pironi (Ferrari); 1983, Patrick Tambay (Ferrari); 1984, Alain Prost (McLaren TAG); 1985, Elio de Angelis (Lotus Renault); 1986, Alain Prost (McLaren TAG); 1987, Nigel Mansell (Williams Honda); 1988, Ayrton Senna (McLaren Honda); 1989, Ayrton Senna (McLaren Honda)

Nigel Mansell: Italian Grand Prix – 1980, did not qualify (Lotus Ford). San Marino Grand Prix – 1981, did not enter; 1982, did not enter; 1983, 12th (Lotus Ford); 1984, retired (Lotus Renault); 1985, 5th (Williams Honda); 1986, retired (Williams Honda); 1987, 1st (Williams Honda); 1988, retired (Williams Judd); 1989, retired (Ferrari)

3 MONACO

Circuit: *Monte Carlo*

The three great motor races are the Indianapolis 500, the Le Mans 24 Hours . . . and the Monaco Grand Prix. Some might dispute that statement: you can find historical and emotional evidence to support almost any case. But these races transcend racing, even sport. They are landmarks on the international, social calendar. The American and sportscar classics, the Blue Riband of Formula One; they do not have to be defined or categorized.

If FISA were presented now with an application to stage a Grand Prix on a circuit corresponding to the dimensions and physical limitations of Monte Carlo it would be laughed out of committee. Overtaking is virtually impossible, the race usually a tedious procession. The ludicrously tight street circuit is also extremely dangerous, even more so with a full field of twenty-six runners. Space is at a premium in the Principality, and Formula One personnel suffer the consequences on and off the track. The pit lane, cramped and chaotic, is potentially lethal. The paddock clings precariously to the quayside. The Press centre is half a mile and a laborious struggle away on the other side of the harbour, in a multi-storey car park.

Ah, but this is Monaco, and this is where the usual rules and requirements go overboard with the champagne corks. There is, after all, only one Monaco.

The Grand Prix is as much a part of Monaco as the Royal Palace, the Casino and the Harbour. To the Formula One World Championship, Monaco means still more. Tradition, old habits and sentiment are a part of it. But so, too, is the money. This Mediterranean festival generates millions of dollars — one recent estimate was $250 million — each year. No drivers' complaints are going to cut off that sort of supply.

And in any case many drivers, including Nigel Mansell, rise to the peculiar challenge of Monte Carlo. The atmosphere, the surroundings, the sense of occasion can inspire the most cynical and hardened of old pedlars.

Monaco is so distinct from all other Grands Prix, the event even starts a day early. First practice is on the Thursday, but not any Thursday. It is always Ascension Thursday. You may care to make a note in your diary: proceedings for the Grand Prix in the year 2000 begin on 11 May. Apart from taking advantage of the holiday, this arrangement conveniently leaves Friday free for fun. The weather isn't reliable at this time of year. Sunbathing can be interrupted by dark clouds rolling down from the mountains. But whatever the weather, there are always parties and ritual nights drinking in the street outside the Tip-Top Club.

Monaco is one of the original World Championship venues. It staged the second of the seven races in 1950, won by Juan Manuel Fangio,

Racing cars and yachts . . . unmistakably Monaco

driving an Alfa Romeo. It was run over 100 laps of the 1·976-mile circuit. The new generation compete over seventy-eight laps of a circuit which is slightly longer at 2·068 miles, but still the shortest on the Grand Prix tour. It is also the slowest.

They were racing here, however, long before the modern concept of Formula One. The first listed winner is W. Williams, of Britain, driving a Bugatti. That was in 1929, and into the 1930s the Bugattis and Alfas dominated until Mercedes Benz took over. When racing resumed after the War, Guiseppe Farina, in a Maserati, celebrated with the 1948 victory.

Monaco disappeared from the Championship map after that 1950 race, although there was a sportscar race in 1952. It returned in 1955, and has been there ever since. Its roll of honour takes you down a memory lane of the sport's greats. Stirling Moss had three victories here, Graham Hill five in seven glorious seasons and Jackie Stewart three. Niki Lauda won in 1975 and '76, while Alain Prost has been the harbour master of the 1980s with four successes.

Two significant absentees from the winners' board are Jim Clark and Nigel Mansell. The tide never went their way. Mansell has twice led and, in 1987, was cruising until that exhaust failure forced him to dock. He still hopes to put the record straight.

Monaco has witnessed some major pile-ups. Nine cars came to grief at Tabac on the first lap in 1950; five were involved in the first corner shunt in 1962; four went at the same corner, St Devote, in 1980. In 1955 Alberto Ascari, driving a Lancia, slid off the road, through the straw bales and into the harbour. He bobbed up to the surface and had only minor injuries. The sad irony is that just a week later he was killed in unofficial testing at Monza. Monaco claimed the life of Lorenzo Bandini in 1967. His Ferrari hit the wooden barriers at the harbour chicane, went into the straw bales and caught fire. He died three days later from his burns. In 1962, a marshal was hit by a car and killed.

The 1984 race was stopped at less than half distance in torrential rain with leader Prost shaking his fist in protest at the ordeal. He and other scorers were awarded half points. Nigel Mansell and Niki Lauda were two distinguished victims of the appalling conditions that day.

In 1988 Nigel was punted out of the action by an impatient Michele Alboreto, but the Italian duly apologized and the pair shook hands. Ayrton Senna, however, went without a word. He had victory in his grasp only to crash at Virage du Portier. He climbed out of his stricken McLaren and walked straight to his apartment, just a few hundred yards away. Some drivers find this more than a tax haven.

Right: *Nigel leads in the wet in 1984*

Monaco is simply *the* special circuit on the calendar. It's the most prestigious race of all. Victory here means so much to any driver. Monte Carlo itself, the setting, the harbour, the topless girls, it all helps create the type of atmosphere only this race has. I love it, always have done, even if the only golf course is on top of a mountain and you can be caught out by the sudden change in weather up there.

The race is as extraordinary as the place. It's the tightest and hardest. Make the smallest of mistakes and you get crucified. Half an inch out can be too much on some corners, because if you hit the barriers hard you've broken your wheel, punctured your tyre or even damaged your suspension. At every corner the barrier or concrete wall or concrete kerb waits for you at the edge of the circuit. There's no escape, so consequently, over the years, there have been some big accidents here.

Monaco is one of the specialist circuits. It's challenging, it's very daunting and I find it fascinating as well. I've had a run of four consecutive front-row positions – one pole and three second places – and a good grid position is absolutely vital. There's very little opportunity for overtaking. Unless a driver in front makes a mistake and gives you a little room to go through, you can be sitting there for lap after lap after lap.

The secret of a good lap is to be at one with the car and flow; you have to flow with every corner. If you're fighting with one corner at Monaco, it's one too many. You need a rhythm here; you don't attack the course. If you can find that rhythm you can have a good weekend. Otherwise . . .

Senna leads into Virage 1988

Monaco is extremely demanding. You are working all the time. The gear changes are fast and furious. If you stay the distance you can be making around 2,500 shifts here. There's no margin for error. Remember you are punching in the gears. There's no synchro; it's a crash box. So you have to keep the revs up. That is of paramount importance. It's a question of feel, of experience.

While I love Monaco, I also hate it. I adore being here, and it is one of the great races in the world. But I've never won it or even had a particularly good result. Fourth is my best finish and that's disappointing. In 1987, when the exhaust broke, I was miles out in front. One of my remaining ambitions is to win this race, and I hope to fulfil it with Ferrari.

Lap of Monte Carlo

Tip-toeing through Station Hairpin

Crossing the start/finish line in sixth, you brake very hard, down to third gear, for the right-hander, St Devote. Here you almost touch the apex of the barrier, and on this circuit we are talking *barriers*. You have to put your right wheel as close as possible to the kerb, with the barrier sitting right on top of it. That's daunting in itself, because the barrier is as high as you are sitting in the car. So straight away you are turning into a corner which is blind, and you're as close to the barrier as you can get.

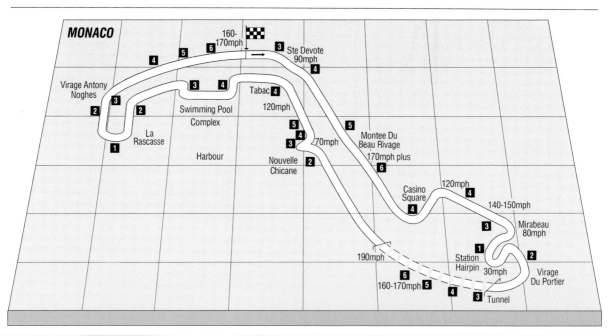

Right: *Full lock for La Rascasse*

Right: *Full lock for La Rascasse*

Below: *Tunnel vision . . . Alain Prost sees victory in 1988*

Through the corner at 90 m.p.h., then accelerating and sliding to the outside barriers. As you're sliding you're changing up to fourth. Then, going up the hill, Montée du Beau Rivage, it's fifth and sixth winding your way – because it's not straight – towards Casino Square. It goes left, right, and left again. Maximum speed on that stretch is upwards of 170 m.p.h.

Down from sixth to fourth, hugging the inside into the square. This corner is dangerous because you are following the barriers and two thirds of the way round the corner the barrier jumps out into the circuit again. If you are too close to the barrier you hit it; if you go too far over you are on to adverse camber, get understeer and you hit the outside barriers.

Round Casino then, hugging the inside in fourth, and switching right to go over the brow, round the right-hander and accelerating to go down the hill. This is one of the most spectacular places to watch, because the car almost takes off here at 120 m.p.h. It jumps from the middle of the circuit to the outside and brushes the barrier.

Down to Mirabeau in fourth at 140 to 150 m.p.h., then braking very hard. There have been some dramatic accidents down here in recent years. There was one involving Patrick Tambay and Martin Brundle, another involving Riccardo Patrese and Philippe Alliot. Tricky, dangerous corner. Third gear, 80 m.p.h., again turning in close to the inside. No barrier here, just a concrete wall.

Keeping it in third gear, almost hitting the rev limiter, down to Station Hairpin, and then standing on the brakes. If not, you're into the Loews Hotel! You are tip-toeing down here. By far the slowest corner, about 30 m.p.h., using first or second gear.

Accelerating hard towards the sea, in second, right and right again at Virage. Again a difficult corner. Barriers on the outside. Sliding out, grazing the barrier. Third, fourth, fifth, sixth through the tunnel, a feature of Monaco that can pose all sorts of problems.

The change of light is extraordinary. You can go from bright sunshine to a tunnel which is lit now, but still has very different light from outside. You also go from fresh air to an area where the air is still and that can affect the aerodynamics of the car. You can lose 20 to 30 per cent of download. In the middle of the tunnel there's a kink which you take flat out at 160 to 170 m.p.h. I have hit the barriers on both sides of the tunnel in sixth, come out in one piece and carried on driving. It's the fastest part of the circuit. I think at the tunnel exit, on maximum boost in the Williams Honda, I was doing more than 190 m.p.h.

Now you're braking hard, down to second for the new chicane (Nouvelle) on the waterfront. A really tight left-right, about 50 m.p.h. Third, fourth, fifth along the straight to Tabac. Down to fourth and

The swimming pool . . . 'I like it, but it's daunting'

again, as close to the inside as you can. Probably 120 m.p.h. here. May not sound much, but when you're committed, with steel guardrails in front of you, that's quick.

Sliding out and heading towards the swimming pool section at about 140 m.p.h. It's a section I like, but also find daunting. On the left you have concrete, on the right barriers on top of a kerb, creating a tunnel effect. Go wrong here and there's no question: it's *big* accident time.

The entrance is tight. Get it wrong and you damage the suspension if you are lucky. If you are unlucky you get hurt yourself. You go in at 120, so committed you can't get the speed down even if you're on the brakes. You might be on the brakes for half a second before you hit the concrete wall. Far better to get it right!

The swimming pool complex, then, is a quick left, quick right, followed by a tight right for which you go down from fourth to third. Short burst into La Rascasse. Braking hard for the left, and then immediately into a tight 180-degree right-hander where you have full lock on. First or second gear, depending on ratios, lots of wheel-spin, sometimes a lot of understeer and you're saying to yourself 'come round, come round'. If the car is set up too well and you've got too much bite on the front, you can actually turn the car straight into the barrier.

Up to Virage Antony Noghes, first to second to third. All adverse camber. Throws you to the outside, where the barriers can grab you. Even when you think you've got the corner absolutely perfect, it can catch your back left-hand side. Sliding the car, getting on the power, smoothly to third, fourth, fifth, sixth, crossing the line at about 160 to 170 m.p.h.

Monaco   Fact file

Circuit length: 2·068 miles, 3·328 km.
Race distance: 78 laps (161·298 miles, 259·584 km.)
Qualifying lap record: Ayrton Senna (McLaren Honda) 1m. 22·308s., in 1989
Race lap record: Alain Prost (McLaren Honda) 1m. 25·501s. at 87·07 m.p.h., in 1989

Winners: 1950, Juan-Manuel Fangio (Alfa Romeo); 1955, Maurice Trintignant (Ferrari); 1956, Stirling Moss (Maserati); 1957, Juan-Manuel Fangio (Maserati); 1958, Maurice Trintignant (Cooper Climax); 1959, Jack Brabham (Cooper Climax); 1960, Stirling Moss (Lotus Climax); 1961 Stirling Moss (Lotus Climax); 1962, Bruce McLaren (Cooper Climax); 1963, Graham Hill (BRM); 1964, Graham Hill (BRM); 1965, Graham Hill (BRM); 1966, Jackie Stewart (BRM); 1967, Denny Hulme (Brabham Repco); 1968, Graham Hill (Lotus Ford); 1969, Graham Hill (Lotus Ford); 1970, Jochen Rindt (Lotus Ford); 1971, Jackie Stewart (Tyrrell Ford); 1972, Jean-Pierre Beltoise (BRM); 1973, Jackie Stewart (Tyrrell Ford); 1974, Ronnie Peterson (Lotus Ford); 1975, Niki Lauda (Ferrari); 1976, Niki Lauda (Ferrari); 1977, Jody Scheckter (Wolf Ford); 1978, Patrick Depailler (Tyrrell Ford); 1979, Jody Scheckter (Ferrari); 1980, Carlos Reutemann (Williams Ford); 1981, Gilles Villeneuve (Ferrari); 1982, Riccardo Patrese (Brabham Ford); 1983, Keke Rosberg (Williams Ford); 1984, Alain Prost (McLaren TAG); 1985, Alain Prost (McLaren TAG); 1986, Alain Prost (McLaren TAG); 1987, Ayrton Senna (Lotus Honda); 1988, Alain Prost (McLaren Honda); 1989, Ayrton Senna (McLaren Honda)

Nigel Mansell: 1981, retired (Lotus Ford); 1982, 4th (Lotus Ford); 1983, retired (Lotus Ford); 1984, accident (Lotus Renault); 1985, 7th (Williams Honda); 1986, 4th (Williams Honda); 1987, retired (Williams Honda); 1988, accident (Williams Judd); 1989, retired (Ferrari)

4 MEXICO

Circuit: **Mexico City** (*Autodromo Hermanos Rodriguez*)

If you seek evidence to argue the democracy of Formula One, merely run you finger down the calendar from Monaco to the next race – Mexico. The circus is transported from the Principality of millionaires and revellers to a city of squalor and sad faces. Here, as in Rio, there is an upper crust. But here the privileged are not so apparent, and here there are no beaches or black and green mountains to camouflage overwhelming reality. The vast country of Mexico has its spectacular beauty and charm, but that is scant consolation for the people of the capital. This is, essentially, a population ensnared by poverty, corruption and recurring disaster. They beg and grovel for the odd peso; they even become road junction fire-eaters knowing they are blazing a trail to certain early death.

The other significant difference between Monaco and Mexico is altitude. From the seafront you have climbed more than 7000 feet. The air is thin, and that gave the turbos a huge advantage over the normally aspirated runners. With less oxygen to draw on, the NAs were losing something like 120 b.h.p. Now they are all NAs and can pant in unison.

Mexico City's infamous smog is another potential hazard, stinging the eyes and blurring vision. It tends, however, to be less of a problem out at the circuit than downtown. After two autumn dates, the revived Mexican Grand Prix now has a slot in late May and provides a stepping stone to North America. Warm sunshine burns through to give pleasant driving and spectating conditions.

Sweeping changes have been made

. . . since 1970

The Mexican Grand Prix featured in the World Championship from 1963 to 1970, but was abandoned as the sport entered an era of greater safety consciousness. Mexican fans had a reputation for being uncontrollable. If they decided they wanted a closer view they simply sat at the edge of the track. And if the organizers couldn't keep people in check, what hope did they have when it came to containing stray dogs?

Jackie Stewart, who had the misfortune of collecting a dog on the track, was more concerned with preserving human life at the 1970 race. He and local driver Pedro Rodriguez appealed to the spectators to move back from the road. Many of the drivers wanted the race to be cancelled, but there were fears that would cause a riot. The start was delayed until eventually the organizers assured the drivers all was well. They had taken out insurance and were covered for any deaths!

The organizers also called in armed troops in an attempt to maintain a semblance of order trackside. In 1966, one duty soldier faced an initiative test when American Ron Bucknum discarded the smouldering seat of his Honda, the consequence of an electrical fire. The bemused soldier ran up to the mysterious object and took what presumably seemed to him the appropriate action: he emptied his gun into it!

The death of Pedro Rodriguez in a sportscar race in Germany in 1971 drained any lingering enthusiasm for the Mexican Grand Prix. His brother, Ricardo, had been killed in practice for the 1962 non-Championship race here.

It was revived in 1986 on the same dried-up lake bed, a public park area close to the airport. But Formula One found considerable changes both to the circuit – now named in honour of the Rodriguez brothers – and in the organization. Cocooned from the desperation of Mexico City life, the paddock and pits provide an excellent working environment for the teams. The garages and pit lane enable them to go about their jobs efficiently and as safely as can be expected.

Not that you can ever totally eliminate danger from racing. In 1988, Philippe Alliot had a massive accident here and debris from his car showered team members at the pit wall. Following that incident and another at Detroit, FISA drew up new regulations on pit wall safety. They called for reinforced concrete walls at least 1·35 metres above track level at new circuits, and inspections of all current circuits.

Above left: *Nigel Mansell snaking to victory in 1987*

Above right: *But heading for another retirement in 1988*

Alliot is by no means the only driver who has come to grief off the final bend here, a terrifying right-hander they exit at 180 m.p.h. or more. In 1987, Nigel Mansell had a shunt on the first day yet still finished qualifying with pole and a record fifteenth consecutive place on the front row of the grid. Not content with that, he went on to win the race, which was run in two parts as a result of Derek Warwick's off at that same last corner.

Nigel's 1986 visit was also eventful, though not ultimately so productive. He was a victim of Montezuma's revenge (a constant threat in these parts) and then had that start-line horror, eventually creeping away in second gear with twenty cars already ahead of him. He was thankful to climb up to fifth place.

That race gave Austrian Gerhard Berger – then driving a Benetton BMW and now Nigel's team-mate at Ferrari – the first win of his Formula One career. The 1988 result had a more routine look about it. Long after Mansell had retired his fading Williams Judd, Alain Prost and Ayrton Senna made it a one-two for the McLaren Honda camp.

Y OU couldn't have a greater contrast in terms of environment than that between Monaco and Mexico. When you switch from one place to the next in consecutive races it's staggering. It's difficult to believe you are actually on the same planet. I like to break up the journey and the time differences by stopping off at Dallas on the way. I stay with friends there, play golf and enjoy the sunshine. Then it's a relatively short hop to Mexico City for business.

The first time we came here, in 1986, I stayed downtown. It's hectic, noisy and, of course, you have the effects of the smog to contend with. There are lots of bars and restaurants in the Zona Rosa area, but this is a city where you have to take constant care over what you eat and drink. You can never be too sure, as I discovered to my cost that year. I tell you, I suffered that weekend.

The traffic is chaotic with battered old vehicles pumping out horrendous fumes. I know one or two people in Formula One who won't risk driving here. The organizers put on a helicopter service from one of the downtown hotels and I took advantage of that. You are into the circuit within a matter of minutes.

In 1987, though, I switched to a big, modern hotel next to the airport and not far from the circuit. In fact, quite a few drivers are staying there now. It means coming into the circuit by road, but overall it's a much better arrangement.

The pit facilities here are very good; among the best anywhere in the world. But the circuit itself poses a lot of problems. It's built on a lake bed, and consequently you couldn't play snap on it because there are no two parts that are the same height. Some sections are

The infamous Peralta Curve brings the cars back to the start/finish line

incredibly bumpy and dangerous. Both driver and car can suffer damage here, as we have seen over the past three years.

The other major problem with the circuit is that it is very dirty, and again that is a danger because it means you can't always get the grip you require. When you are committed on a flying lap you like to know you have a reasonable chance of staying on the road! The cars sweep the track during the course of the day, and eventually it's not too bad. But the following morning you return to find more dust and rubbish. The smog doesn't help, of course. Nor does the altitude. For many, many reasons, then, driving here is made a very difficult job.

You will gather from all this that I don't exactly look forward to coming here, but it is precisely the sort of situation that tests the attitude and the professionalism of a racing driver. We do race all over the world, and this is a Championship round. You have to be positive and not allow any of the problems or circumstances to affect your approach to the race. That, at least, is the way I go into it, and I suppose you could say I've proved the point by winning here.

Lap of Mexico City

Across the start/finish line you are flying because you have come out of Peralta Curve, the fifth gear, flat-out right-hander, at 180 m.p.h. and ahead of you is the long main straight. Up to sixth and hard on. This is where the turbos really used to murder the normally aspirated cars. The twisty bits bring down the average speed of the circuit into

But not for Ayrton Senna this time

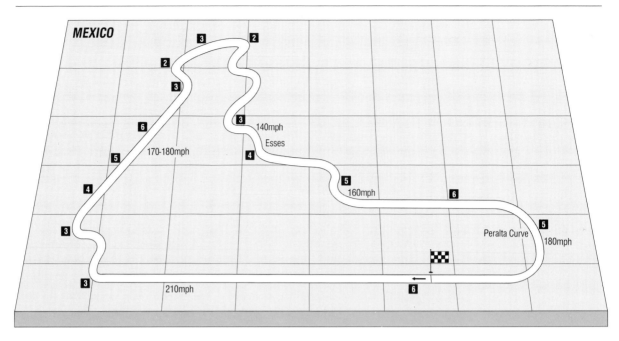

the medium category, but this straight is one of the fastest in the world. Because the air is so thin up here you can get up to speeds of 210 m.p.h. before you come to the chicane.

Obviously there is a lot of overtaking at this section. If you have the power advantage, no problem at all. But at the end of the main straight you're braking hard and changing down to third for this complex chicane. You have a right-hander, then a left-hander, and this is where extra care is needed. There is only one line in Mexico. By that I mean a foot either side of it and you are in dust and rubbish and off you go. No second chance. That's how little grip there is.

You come out of this section at the right-hander, and onto the back straight. Back up through the gears. Third, to fourth, to fifth, to sixth. Here we are approaching speeds of 170 to 180 m.p.h., but coming up next is a long sequence of bends. In fact, there are ten of them in all, flowing together in one great movement.

So braking down to third gear at the end of the back straight to begin the sequence with a left-hander. Second gear for the right-hander, up to third and down to second again for the next right. We are now into the flowing movement – or at least hopefully we are – and it's essential to maintain the rhythm. Lose that and you lose time. Worse still, you can be off the track.

Up to third and fourth to go through the Esses. These can be very tricky bends. They are very fast. You are sweeping through them at about 140 m.p.h. Again, stay on line. Get too far off line and lose grip at that speed means serious trouble. The last bend before you come onto the straight, a left-hander, is flat out in fifth and taken at about 160 m.p.h.

Another point where you really do have to take care to stay on line. Apart from the lack of grip here it's incredibly bumpy. I have had one or two nasty moments here and I can assure you, it's no joke. There is no room for error whatsoever. Come through there onto

Eating time for the troops

another straight, flat out in sixth, before that final corner, the Peralta Curve.

You are travelling at upwards of 180 m.p.h. and only dabbing the brakes a little, shifting down to fifth and then going flat out round the right-hander. As if the speed isn't enough, there are a couple of bumps in the middle of the corner you have to beware of. They can so unsettle the car as to make you have an accident.

It's challenging, yes, and from a spectator's point of view it is very spectacular. But I have to be honest and say I don't particularly like it. It really isn't too safe. In fact, I would go so far as to say it is one of the most dangerous corners in the world of motor racing today. There are a lot of daunting, nasty corners, but this one is something else.

I had that bad one in 1987, so I can speak from experience. When you're having an accident there it's frightening. Philippe Alliot had a massive one in 1988, and he was very lucky to be able to walk away from it. I believe we all earn our money round that corner alone. You're just happy to come out of it in one piece and lunge for the line to complete the lap.

Mexico City   Fact file

Circuit length: 2·747 miles, 4·421 km.
Race distance: 68 laps (186·796 miles, 300·628 km.)
Qualifying lap record: Ayrton Senna (Lotus Renault) 1m. 16·990s., in 1986
Race lap record: Alain Prost (McLaren Honda) 1m. 18·608s. at 125·808 m.p.h., in 1988

Winners: 1963, Jim Clark (Lotus Climax); 1964, Dan Gurney (Brabham Climax); 1965, Richie Ginther (Honda); 1966, John Surtees (Cooper Maserati); 1967, Jim Clark (Lotus Ford); 1968, Graham Hill (Lotus Ford); 1969, Denny Hulme (McLaren Ford); 1970, Jacky Ickx (Ferrari); 1986, Gerhard Berger (Benetton BMW); 1987, Nigel Mansell (Williams Honda); 1988, Alain Prost (McLaren Honda)

Nigel Mansell: 1986, 5th (Williams Honda); 1987, 1st (Williams Honda); 1988, retired (Williams Judd)

5 USA

Circuit: **Phoenix**

It is generally accepted that a race in the United States is essential for the credibility of the Formula One World Championship. Indianapolis appears in the records as one of the original seven title venues, even if it was a distinctly domestic affair. The 500 held its slot through to 1960 but by then a genuine Grand Prix, with genuine Grand Prix contenders, was appearing on American soil. The 1959 US Grand Prix at Sebring had Stirling Moss on pole and Bruce McLaren on the winner's rostrum. In 1960, at Riverside, Moss took not only pole but the race as well.

The US Grand Prix found a proper home at Watkins Glen the following year, and remained in residence there until 1980. From 1976 it had a new handle: USA East Grand Prix. That was because a second American race – USA West Grand Prix – had taken to the streets of Long Beach. In 1982 there were actually three American races – at Long Beach, Detroit and Las Vegas. The Championship was booming Stateside. Or was it?

The fact is that Formula One has an identity crisis in America. The campaign for approval in a land more at ease with CART racing hasn't been helped by its chopping and changing of venues in the 1980s. FISA has been seen more as a bunch of mercenary opportunists after a fast buck than a sporting organization. They had a couple of spins with the high rollers at Las Vegas and one ride in and out of Dallas. Detroit became a more regular jaunt, but after seven not always magnificent years the show moved out of Motown, too.

When Detroit pulled out of the market for a 1989 race Formula One spread its net for a replacement. There were plenty of eager takers over in Europe, but the sport needed to maintain a foothold in the States. The USA was even given a date on the calendar – 4 June, venue to be announced. There was talk of a return to Long Beach, even the Glen. But only talk. The real discussions centred around Road Atlanta, in Georgia, Laguna Seca, in California, and then Phoenix, Arizona.

The uncertainty merely fed the cynicism of the purists, those who were adamant the race should never have left the Glen. It wasn't a case of decrying all street circuits. Long Beach was well accepted, its passing lamented. But there are street circuits and street circuits. The Glen was something else again. A real circuit.

Watkins Glen is also a circuit that has known tragedy. Frenchman François Cevert was killed here, the scene of his only Grand Prix win, in practice for the 1973 race. A year later Austrian Helmuth Koinigg was killed during the race, only his second Grand Prix.

When Formula One left downtown Long Beach and Caesar's Palace parking lot, Las Vegas, it made its American base in Detroit. The one diversion, and then *en route* from Michigan, was through Dallas in 1984.

Above: *Mansell beginning his first full season for Lotus, tracked by World Champion and race winner, Alan Jones, Long Beach, 1981*

Right: *Jones on the victory trail at Watkins Glen, 1980*

Left: *Dallas,
1984 . . . workers patch
up the track*

Right: *. . . and Nigel
receives attention after
vainly trying to push his
car across the line*

Texas promised a warm reception and the hosts were as good as their word. Temperatures rose into the 100s, the track crumbled. Amid quite bizarre race day scenes, workmen patched up the offending areas with quick-setting cement and the show was saved.

Keke Rosberg managed to miss the walls and the parked racing cars to win the race. Nigel Mansell didn't make it to the line, despite a valiant attempt to push his stricken Lotus along the final, tantalizing stretch of road. He collapsed through heat and exhaustion yet came round to be told he was classified sixth.

The American races haven't been his most productive. He began his full-time job with Lotus at Long Beach in 1981, qualified an encouraging seventh but limped out of the race after twenty-five laps. He closed the season with fourth place at Las Vegas. His only other point before that Dallas race was picked up at Detroit, in 1983, when the normally aspirated runners made their last stand against the turbos. Michele Alboreto led the way in the Tyrrell Ford, followed by Rosberg (Williams Ford) and John Watson (McLaren Ford). Detroit 1984 brought Nigel only a fine after a startline pile-up.

His switch to Williams Honda gave him more optimism but not much more luck. In 1985 he started on the front row, only to fall foul of the notorious Turn Three, while team-mate Keke Rosberg went on to win. In 1986 he was again on the front row alongside Ayrton Senna's Lotus. He led during the early part of the race, but his pace was checked by braking problems and he was content to settle for fifth place.

Nigel beat the Brazilian to pole in 1987 and again the opening exchanges looked promising. This time, though, cramp sabotaged his plans, and it was all he could do to hang on for another fifth place. He qualified sixth with the Williams Judd in 1988, and managed just eighteen laps before electrical problems forced him out of the action.

Despite those results Mansell was always philosophical about the Detroit circuit. Others weren't. Alain Prost, for instance, openly and vehemently condemned the circuit as 'crazy . . . a joke . . . no place to hold a World Championship race.' Every year he came back, but every year he declared his dissatisfaction.

The Detroit organizers laid their circuit in the downtown area, along the Detroit River and around the Renaissance Center, the complex of business and commerce towers pointing the way upwards for a city long entombed in the depths of despair.

The Grand Prix was a part of the new Detroit, a symbol of the vibrant, enterprising future. It would generate money and optimism; it would give the city stature and fun. The good folk of Detroit threw themselves into the spirit of the thing. Grand Prix week was party week. Much as in Adelaide, the state of the Championship didn't seem to matter too much. Here was an event and a festival in its own right. 'The Champion' here was the winner of the previous Detroit Grand Prix. I doubt the majority of the punters could have named the world title holder.

There can be no denying the organization improved with every year. The operation became slicker, more assured. The track surface, dotted with manhole covers, was always bumpy and slippery. Along the riverside the road was constantly subsiding; at the ninety degree turns it would break up and trap even the most experienced. And always waiting to devour the unfortunate were those unforgiving concrete walls. Practice sessions were frequently held up while crippled cars were hoisted out of the way. Gradually, though, resurfacing ironed out some of the bumps and the removal men quickened their step.

The anti-Detroit lobby remained forceful, however, and when redevelopment plans were drawn up for the riverside area it seemed the race would be rehoused on Belle Isle, a leisure retreat on the river, just a few minutes by car or boat from downtown. But pressure from environmentalists forced the city to drop that idea. It would have to be the streets, after all. FISA insisted on vastly improved facilities, Detroit would not comply and decided to put on CART racing instead.

Many Detroiters had had enough of those 'high-falutin' elitist Europeans'. Others said they would be glad to see the back of Formula One and have names of drivers they could pronounce. Others – notably at Ford – might not have shared those views.

The rulers of Formula One were certainly not gloating. Motor city was regarded as a vital shop window. Worse still, there was no obvious replacement. Road Atlanta had its supporters, Britain's John Watson among them. He had raced Jaguar's IMSA series sportscar there. 'I think it would make a good Grand Prix circuit,' he said. 'It may require some work, but the potential is there.'

Others favoured Laguna Seca, and circuit chiefs underlined their ambitions by resurfacing the track. Laguna's critics, however, insisted that there was inadequate access and insufficient accommodation in the area. Suddenly the hot tip was Phoenix, even more convenient, after all, for a race just one week after the Mexican Grand Prix.

Phoenix has developed a reputation as a thriving, ambitious community and sport is seen as a crucial vehicle for its continued advance. The city has bought its own basketball team and, at enormous expense, the pro-football team franchise from St Louis Cardinals.

Motor racing already has solid support in the area. There is a successful oval track and a Firebird road course. But a group of businessmen, led by Howard Pynn, clinched a five-year deal (with an option of a further five years) to run the USA Grand Prix on a new downtown street circuit. They pledged 2·9 million dollars to prepare the track and a further 1·6 million dollars annually for its upkeep.

The organisers mapped out a 2·2 mile course, inevitably featuring a succession of 90-degree turns. But Phoenix is blessed with wide streets – up to 20 metres – so that speeds and overtaking should not be as restricted as in Detroit. There were confident predictions of 100 m.p.h.-plus laps. FISA officials were impressed with the safety plans, hotels, and the space to accommodate a race crowd and their cars.

The one fear concerned the weather. Early June temperatures in this desert city often top 100 degrees. The general feeling was that from 1990 onwards the race should be held in the spring, possibly following the Brazilian Grand Prix.

THERE is no doubt that it is important for Formula One to have a race in the United States. I'm sure everyone sees that. And if you are in the United States, where better or more appropriate than the centre of the motor industry. The fact is, of course, that the Detroit circuit was not the most popular around and not many drivers will be sorry to leave it behind.

It would be less than honest of me to say I didn't agree with some of the comments made about Detroit. People tend to bracket Monaco and Detroit together. Both street circuits, both slow circuits. But at Detroit you have only a couple of good corners, the rest are ninety-degree turns. Some of the corners are also blind and dangerous. At Monaco you have more genuine racing corners. There's also less concrete at Monaco, and you tend not to get hurt so easily in the Principality.

The towers of the Renaissance Center look down on Mansell, Senna and co., Detroit, '86

The purists have basically never had any time for Detroit, and I can appreciate their point of view. Yes, it was narrow, unpredictable, totally uncompromising and often treacherous. There was only one line and if you didn't keep to it you were in trouble. Even when you

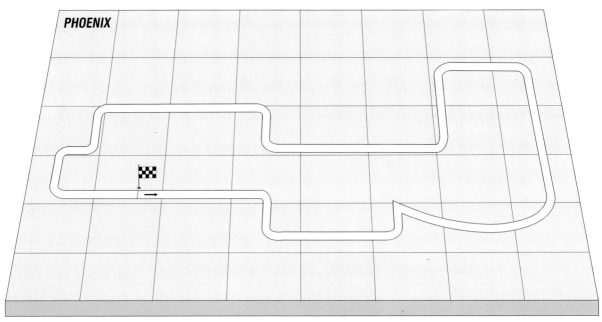

thought things were going well you'd suddenly find yourself facing horrendous problems.

But for all its faults it seemed to me there was no point going on about them. Here was another Grand Prix circuit, another World Championship race. My results weren't too good there, but I never allowed that to deflate me and never talked myself out of it.

I was frankly sorry to see Detroit go. From a driving point of view it did present its own, very individual challenge. From a personal point of view I like the area, I have made some good friends there, and within a short distance of the circuit there are three magnificent Championship golf courses.

Wherever and whenever we race in America, this is one part of the world I definitely enjoy. I'm sure Phoenix will be no exception. When the race is back-to-back with another race, say Canada or Mexico, you might get the opportunity to take a bit of a break, play some golf, see some friends. The workload, though, can be very heavy. Especially so if Mexico, America and Canada are all in the space of three weeks. For mechanics and drivers alike, it can be very hectic.

Below left: Detroit . . .
'narrow, unpredictable,
uncompromising and
often treacherous'

But that's the way it is in motor racing. If you get the results it's amazing how you forget the hours of toil, the problems and the setbacks. I've won races in Canada and Mexico, so now I'm after an American win to complete this particular set.

United States Fact file

Winners: 1959, Sebring, Bruce McLaren (Cooper Climax); 1960, Riverside, Stirling Moss (Lotus Climax); 1961, Watkins Glen, Innes Ireland (Lotus Climax); 1962, Watkins Glen, Jim Clark (Lotus Climax); 1963, Watkins Glen, Graham Hill (BRM); 1964, Watkins Glen, Graham Hill (BRM); 1965, Watkins Glen, Graham Hill (BRM); 1966, Watkins Glen, Jim Clark (Lotus BRM); 1967, Watkins Glen, Jim Clark (Lotus Ford); 1968, Watkins Glen, Jackie Stewart (Matra Ford); 1969, Watkins Glen, Jochen Rindt (Lotus Ford); 1970, Watkins Glen, Emerson Fittipaldi (Lotus Ford); 1971, Watkins Glen, François Cevert (Tyrrell Ford); 1972, Watkins Glen, Jackie Stewart (Tyrrell Ford); 1973, Watkins Glen, Ronnie Peterson (Lotus Ford); 1974, Watkins Glen, Carlos Reutemann (Brabham Ford); 1975, Watkins Glen, Niki Lauda (Ferrari); 1976, Long Beach, Clay Regazzoni (Ferrari); Watkins Glen, James Hunt (McLaren Ford); 1977, Long Beach, Mario Andretti (Lotus Ford); Watkins Glen, James Hunt (McLaren Ford); 1978, Long Beach, Carlos Reutemann (Ferrari); Watkins Glen, Carlos Reutemann (Ferrari); 1979, Long Beach, Gilles Villeneuve (Ferrari); Watkins Glen, Gilles Villeneuve (Ferrari); 1980, Long Beach, Nelson Piquet (Brabham Ford); Watkins Glen, Alan Jones (Williams Ford); 1981, Long Beach, Alan Jones (Williams Ford); Las Vegas, Alan Jones (Williams Ford); 1982, Long Beach, Niki Lauda (McLaren Ford); Detroit, John Watson (McLaren Ford); Las Vegas, Michele Alboreto (Tyrrell Ford); 1983, Long Beach, John Watson (McLaren Ford); Detroit, Michele Alboreto (Tyrrell Ford); 1984, Detroit, Nelson Piquet (Brabham BMW); Dallas, Keke Rosberg (Williams Honda); 1985, Detroit, Keke Rosberg (Williams Honda); 1986, Detroit, Ayrton Senna (Lotus Renault); 1987, Detroit, Ayrton Senna (Lotus Honda); 1988, Detroit, Ayrton Senna (McLaren Honda)

Nigel Mansell: 1981, Long Beach, accident (Lotus Ford); Las Vegas, 4th (Lotus Ford); 1982, Long Beach, 7th (Lotus Ford); Detroit, retired (Lotus Ford); Las Vegas, retired (Lotus Ford); 1983, Long Beach, 12th (Lotus Ford); Detroit, 6th (Lotus Ford); 1984, Detroit, retired (Lotus Renault); Dallas, 6th (Lotus Renault); 1985, Detroit, accident (Williams Honda); 1986, 5th (Williams Honda); 1987, 5th (Williams Honda); 1988, retired (Williams Judd)

6 CANADA

Circuit: **Montreal** *(Circuit Gilles Villeneuve)*

A convoy of magnificent trucks heads north, through the United States and into Canada. They carry the cars and equipment to the next show. The drivers (some have been back to Europe, some have taken a break on this side of the Atlantic) fly in from various points. Wherever they've been, whichever way they've travelled, they're content to be converging on Montreal.

The Canadian Grand Prix was elbowed out of the 1987 World Championship in a monster row over sponsorship and promotion rights. Its return was all the more welcome since it came immediately after Mexico on the calendar. City and circuit make this one of the most popular weekends of the season.

The business and commercial areas have the appearance and feel of almost any big North American city, but into the older quarters the French flavour becomes more evident. There's also a thriving China Town. If lobster suits your palate you've come to the right place. A Lobster Festival conveniently coincides with Grand Prix time. If you have a taste for flesh spots, you'll find they come up to a fairly high standard, too. Italian Teo Fabi sampled both the lobster and the floor show in 1986, and suffered for his overindulgence the following day. He was taken ill at the wheel of his Benetton BMW during practice and careered off the track into a barrier.

Canada arrived on the World Championship tour in 1967. Mosport was the first venue and, apart from a couple of excursions to Mont Tremblant, the race made its home there until 1977. By then, however, there were growing protests about the Ontario circuit. It was said to be too bumpy, outdated, dangerous.

The solution was found on a new site at Montreal. Or, to be more precise, an island in the St Lawrence. To one side the river, to the other the Seaway. The centre of the city is just a short Metro, road or boat trip away. Isle Notre Dame had, by then, become accustomed to the big occasion. Expo 67 was staged here; the rowing events at the 1976 Olympic Games were held here. Constructions for both events remain in evidence.

The task of designing a Grand Prix circuit was entrusted to English-born Roger Peart, who took advantage of the road network serving the Expo pavilions. Revisions have been made over the years, and for the 1988 comeback race there were new pit facilities and a new position for the startline. Like Montreal itself, the circuit appeals to the drivers, presenting as it does a variety of corners and challenges.

Gilles Villeneuve, the dazzling French Canadian, won the first Championship race here and the circuit was given his name after his death in 1982. That was a tragic year for Formula One and for Canada

Circuit Gilles Villeneuve . . . 'nice setting, a test of driving ability'

in particular. The young Italian Ricardo Paletti was killed on the Montreal grid when his car ran into the back of Didier Pironi's stalled Ferrari. Mercifully, there hasn't been a fatal Grand Prix racing accident since, though Elio de Angelis was killed in testing at the Paul Ricard circuit in 1986.

In 1980 seven cars were involved in a pile-up shortly after the start. The title contenders, Australian Alan Jones and Brazilian Nelson Piquet, exchanged accusations over the incident. There never was any love lost between them. They started again, Piquet's engine blew, while the Williams driver went on to win the race and the Championship.

Jones had also won here the previous year, but the 1979 Canadian Grand Prix will be best remembered for the actions of a man who didn't win and didn't even compete. Instead he walked away from it all. Just after the start of practice Niki Lauda decided he'd had enough of racing and quit. (He returned to the track in 1982, and in 1984 won his third world title.)

Nigel Mansell had nothing to show for his first three races in Montreal. In 1982 he broke his wrist here, an injury which affected him for the rest of the season. In 1984, his last year with Lotus, he picked up a point. In 1985, his first year with Williams, he picked up another. In 1986 he was interested only in rich pickings. He dominated qualifying, dominated the race and took nine points. In 1988 it was, alas, the familiar story of retirement.

I haven't always had the best of fortune in Montreal, but that's not to take anything away from the place. Most of the drivers look forward to coming here. Montreal itself is great, Canadians are very friendly, and there are some fantastic golf courses in Canada. I like to get here early, play a few rounds and relax before we get down to practice.

The circuit itself is one of the more pleasant ones in the world. It's in a nice setting, and it also sets the driver a fair test of his ability. There are some tough corners, corners that can catch you out. The fact that most drivers like this circuit and respond to it made my 1986 win all the more satisfying.

They've made tremendous changes here, and for that we should congratulate both the Canadian organizers and FISA. The pit facilities are now second to none. You cannot overemphasize the importance of good pits. This is serious work. The mechanics must have the room to do their jobs properly and safely. Congested pits can be deathtraps.

The circuit has a lot of character. You have an interesting mix of quick and slow corners. The Pits Hairpin is very distinctive. There are some fast stretches broken up by difficult kinks and demanding Esses. Overall, it's a medium-speed circuit.

As at Imola, fuel consumption was a problem for the turbos. The combination of corners, all the braking and accelerating, are bound to take their toll on supplies. Now we all have normally aspirated engines it will, I hope, ensure good racing. This is, more than anything, a true drivers' circuit, and I'd like to think that will be evident in the years to come.

Left and below: *Pits Hairpin . . . good viewing point for fans and drivers alike*

Lap of Montreal

The start/finish line used to be on the straight just after the Pits Hairpin, but now it's up at the other end, just before it turns at the Island Hairpin and comes back down again. There are still more changes planned because in 1988 we were taking the last chicane before the new pits and start/finish line flat in fifth.

That was far too quick, so they were rightly talking in terms of putting in a second- or third-gear chicane there instead. It was generally accepted that would be much better because it would probably become an overtaking place which would be good for the fans and drivers alike. It would also be far, far safer.

Into the Island Hairpin you are down to second gear or even first, depending on your car's set-up. It's a slow, slow right-hander, about 30 to 40 m.p.h. Then accelerating and quickly up to second, third, fourth and fifth towards the first chicane round the back of the circuit.

Below left and right: *Canadian Grand Prix, 1988 . . . turning in . . . and hugging the kerb*

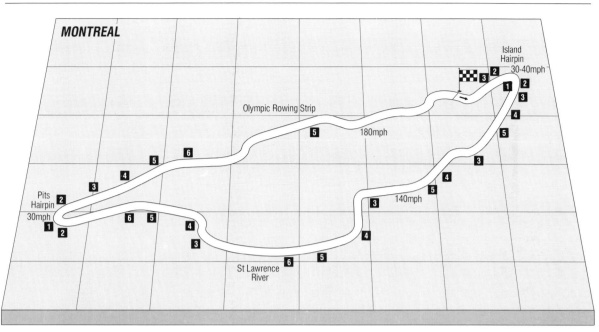

MONTREAL

Island
Hairpin
30-40mph

Olympic Rowing Strip

180mph

Pits
Hairpin
30mph

140mph

St Lawrence
River

Here we start a difficult complex of chicanes. There are two sets of them, placed between concrete walls. The kerbs are high on this circuit so you can't afford to hit them. You come down from fifth to third to take the first sequence of chicanes. Accelerating, fourth, and then, before the track curves round to the right, you're in fifth.

You are taking this curve flat out. Now this is a blind corner, so just consider the prospect for the driver. A sling-shot through this blind corner at 140 m.p.h., into perhaps 100 yards of straight road before you are into a left-hand chicane. If anything goes wrong or the car spins you can imagine the consequences. Make no mistake, these circuits can be very dangerous.

Into this next chicane you are down to third gear. Through the left, and you're already into fourth before the next right. Up to fifth and sixth, on into the concrete tunnel before you come to a chicane which is quite fast. It's third gear. A quick flick right, a quick flick left. Fourth gear as you are sliding, coming out of the corner, again between concrete walls. In certain sections here there is more wall than barrier.

Accelerating down the back straight into fifth, into sixth and approaching the Pits Hairpin. This is the tightest corner on the circuit, and coming into it is a good overtaking place. You've been up to 180 m.p.h., and you're coming right down to second or even first gear and about 30 m.p.h.

It's a good viewing point not only for the fans but also for the drivers. You can see other cars coming down as you're accelerating away. You can work out whether you're pulling away from anyone or being caught. There aren't many circuits where you can see what's happening in front and behind you like this. It's a good corner, I like it a lot.

Wheel-spinning out of it. Second, third, fourth, fifth and sixth, onto a long straight which has two chicanes, taken flat in sixth and fifth. The old start/finish line was on the stretch between Pits Hairpin and the first of these chicanes. There are bumps. You rise a little, go over one bump, you flick right. Then you have to flick left, then right again. You are taking these at something like 180 m.p.h.

Needless to say, either side of these corners are concrete walls, so care is needed. Equally, you have to be as quick as possible if you want to be competitive. It's very easy to get it wrong, as people have shown over the years by clipping the kerb one side and being thrown across the circuit into the wall at the other. You don't take it lightly when you're flat in sixth.

Onto the next chicane, just before the new pits, which, as I've said, we were taking flat in fifth in 1988. Almost everyone agreed it was too fast and too dangerous, so hopefully it will be a more sensible proposition in future and a safer last corner of the circuit.

One of the best circuits in the Championship, then. A lot of challenges. You have to be precise and position the car accurately. You have to manage your car very carefully. Do that and the chances are you'll have a good Canadian Grand Prix.

Rich pickings . . . Nigel dominates in 1986

Montreal Fact file

Circuit length: 2·728 miles, 4·390 km. (previously 2·74 miles, 4·410 km)

Race distance: 69 laps (188·219 miles, 302·91 km.; previously 189·06 miles, 304·29 km.

Qualifying lap record: Ayrton Senna (McLaren Honda) 1m. 21·681s., in 1988. Previously, Nigel Mansell (Williams Honda) 1m. 24·118s., in 1986

Race lap record: Ayrton Senna (McLaren Honda) 1m. 24·973s. at 115·567 m.p.h., in 1988. Previously, Nelson Piquet (Williams Honda) 1m. 25·443s. at 115·456 m.p.h., in 1986

Winners: 1978, Gilles Villeneuve (Ferrari); 1979, Alan Jones (Williams Ford); 1980, Alan Jones (Williams Ford); 1981, Jacques Laffite (Ligier Matra); 1982, Nelson Piquet (Brabham BMW); 1983, René Arnoux (Ferrari); 1984, Nelson Piquet (Brabham BMW); 1985, Michele Alboreto (Ferrari); 1986, Nigel Mansell (Williams Honda); 1988, Ayrton Senna (McLaren Honda)

Nigel Mansell: 1981, accident (Lotus Ford); 1982, accident (Lotus Ford); 1983, retired (Lotus Ford); 1984, 6th (Lotus Renault); 1985, 6th (Williams Honda); 1986, 1st (Williams Honda); 1988, retired (Williams Judd)

7 FRANCE

Circuit: **Le Castellet** (Paul Ricard)

The business of North America behind now, it's back to the other side of the Atlantic for the main part of the European season. Over the next three months the Formula One train will zig-zag across the continent, stopping at eight venues *en route*, a schedule which will account for half the championship.

First stop is France, a country that was on board for the opening title trek in 1950. That year Reims was the circuit, one Juan-Manuel Fangio the winner in an Alfa Romeo. Rouen was given an occasional piece of the action in the years that followed, and Le Mans staged the 1967 Grand Prix to end the Reims connection. Rouen took 1968, and Clermont-Ferrand emerged for 1969 and 1970.

But by now the safety movement was underway. Drivers were demanding higher circuit standards, and the sport's authorities were gradually − if in some cases reluctantly − coming to terms with their requirements. Paul Ricard, he of liquid refreshment fame, satisfied modern expectations and his own ambition by creating a circuit up on the bleached rocks of Provence, Southern France. It was regarded as safe yet challenging, and was equipped with splendid facilities.

Ricard staged the Grand Prix in 1971 and thereafter shared the honour, first with Clermont-Ferrand, and then with Dijon. When FISA decided on a policy of one-country-one-track, Dijon was dropped and, since 1985, Ricard has been the permanent home of the French Grand Prix.

Provence in high summer is a kaleidoscope: all movement, sparkle and fun. The Mediterranean resorts are bristling, the market places buzzing. Multi-coloured people in multi-coloured garments; pouting and posing. There's real Provence too. Humble fishing boats, boules and beautiful old churches. And inland, away from Bandol and Cassis and the waves of humanity, are rolling fields of lavender.

Inland, too, is the ancient village of Le Castellet. A quota of inevitable souvenirs and trinkets haven't diminished the quality or appeal of this little hilltop gem. Ricard went higher and a little further inland still to find the barren site for his dream circuit. Marseilles is twenty-one miles west of here, Toulon seventeen miles to the east. In keeping with the image of this advanced facility, Ricard had an airstrip laid alongside the circuit.

Jackie Stewart won the first Grand Prix at Ricard, and in 1980 victory went to Alan Jones in the Williams. That result gave particular satisfaction to the British camp. They had beaten the Ligiers in their own backyard, and Jones went on, of course, to become Williams' first champion.

The next race here, in 1982, was very much a French affair. In fact, it was almost civil war. Renault pair René Arnoux and Alain Prost dominated and Prost, as No. 1 driver, waited for his partner to make

Above: *Paul Ricard's dream come true*

Right: *. . . in the scorched hills of Provence*

way. He waited in vain. Arnoux maintained he'd seen no instructions to allow Prost through and gleefully took the flag. Prost was incensed, a reaction which merely fuelled Arnoux's joy. The following year Arnoux was with Ferrari.

The 1983 race presented Prost with no such problem. He won comfortably, yet although he and Renault celebrated, Ricard was hardly an arena of national pride and passion. The Grand Prix was held in April. The resorts and campsites were virtually empty that cool weekend, and few felt the compulsion to venture up the twisting roads to Ricard. Now the race has a regular slot in early July and temperatures are usually in the eighties or higher.

Up to and including the 1985 French Grand Prix, the length of Ricard was 3·61 miles, more than a mile of that accounted for by the Mistral Straight. In 1986, however, the circuit was hurriedly changed. A section was cut out and the Mistral considerably reduced in length. Now Ricard measures 2·369 miles.

The alterations followed Elio de Angelis's fatal accident during testing, and the subsequent controversy over safety standards. What an irony. Just fifteen years on, the circuit built to meet modern specifications was the subject of a searching examination. That, in itself, provides a measure of the development in this sport. What, however, compounded the drivers' anger that day in May was the response to the emergency situation. Marshals were said to be dressed in T-shirts and shorts. It is estimated the Italian was trapped eight minutes before being released and there was a further lengthy wait for a helicopter. He died the following day in hospital.

Many drivers were still unimpressed with the marshals at the Grand Prix. The fire services didn't ease their discomfort when they drove into the pitlane entrance, pointed the hose at Philippe Streiff's burning Tyrrell – and looked back in horror as the foam came out of the rear.

I have very mixed emotions about Ricard. So much seems to have happened here. I have good memories because I have won a couple of races here in recent seasons, and it was on this circuit back in 1979 that I first drove a Formula One car. That was my test drive with Lotus, and the following year I made my Grand Prix debut with the team.

But too many memories of this place are bad ones. I had a horrendous accident here in 1985. I was approaching the end of the Mistral, on the way to Signes, at 200 m.p.h. when I had a rear tyre blow. I was hit on the head by a torn-off wheel, had concussion and missed the race. But in the circumstances that was nothing. I was lucky to be in one piece because that was a big, big accident.

Just before the start of the 1986 season we were testing here and things looked all set for the Championship. Frank Williams left ahead of us in his hire car, but crashed on the way to the airport. He was very seriously ill, and although he pulled through he is confined to a wheelchair. A couple of months later came Elio's accident. He was my team-mate at Lotus, a great driver and a gentleman. We were good friends.

Ricard is not a circuit to be taken lightly, and that was especially so in its original form. The Mistral then was too long. The corners past the pits were very fast and very dangerous. Now the Mistral is shorter and that part past the pits, where Elio had his accident, has gone. The circuit is better and safer, but the sad thing is that someone's life had to be claimed before the changes were made.

I do actually find this a good circuit, a challenging circuit and at least I have happier times to recall here. I won the race in 1986, when we made two excellent tyre changes and beat Alain Prost. In 1987 I didn't make a second stop, paced it carefully and beat my team-mate

Left: *Victory charge, 1987*

Right: *Victory champagne, 1986*

Nelson Piquet, who did make a second stop. Those were two very satisfying wins.

Tyre changes can be vital here. It can be very hot, very demanding. It's also difficult to get the car balanced just right. You need enough downforce to get through the corners as quickly as possible, but you don't want too much drag down the Mistral if you are going to be competitive. So you have to take all that into account and find a sensible compromise. That, though, is all part of the challenge and it's a challenge I generally enjoy.

Lap of Le Castellet

Coming to the start/finish line out of the right-hander, Virage du Pont, you are changing up from second or third gear, depending on your ratios. It's very important to make the correct choice of ratios for your needs. Quickly up through the gears: third, fourth, fifth and sixth. Along the straight in front of the pits.

Now we have a tight turn not far beyond the pits, taking us into the new section of the track. When it was first used there was a lot of concern that we might have a pile-up here, but fortunately that hasn't proved to be the case.

So from sixth gear you're braking down hard, very hard, to second gear for the right-hander at Verrene. The road bends a little to the left before turning right again onto the Mistral. It's a very short stretch, but it can cause trouble. You have to beware the ripple strips on this circuit, on the inside and the outside. They will break your suspension. One or two drivers and cars have come to grief that way. It's a much better idea here to stay on the black bits!

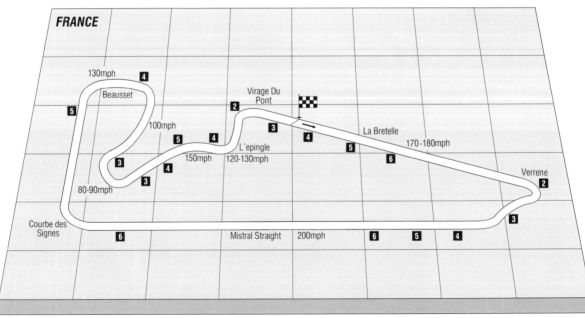

Gerhard Berger seeks that vital momentum for the Mistral

Very important, then, to be precise through this new part, but equally important to take the second right-hander as quickly as possible because this will dictate your exit speed and in turn your speed down the Mistral Straight. So it's third gear for this right, hopefully coming out with the sort of momentum you want for what is still a long straight. I cannot overemphasize how crucial that is.

Third, fourth, fifth, sixth gear, pushing hard up the Mistral. You can reach 200 m.p.h., but so much here depends on the strength and direction of the wind. If it's behind you, 200-plus is possible. If it's against you 200 may be out of reach. The wind really is a significant factor. So much so that you have to change gear ratios to deal with it. The wind can change to that extent from morning to afternoon.

Whatever the wind is doing along that straight, though, you're going to be fast and you are still in sixth, virtually flat out for the right-hander at Signes. It was coming into here I had that accident in 1985. A frightening experience, I don't mind admitting. It's an incredible corner, an experience in itself.

Coming out of Signes you want to hold on very tightly and push it along before you come up to the horseshoe, which is named after the neaby village of Le Beausset. It is a double right-hander. Quite a remarkable corner. Very fast – up to about 130 m.p.h. – and a real test. It's the corner where your tyres are also put to the test. They can be destroyed because you're going so quickly you start sliding. You can lose rubber and speed. In so many ways this is a critical part of the circuit.

You go into the corner in fifth, and change down to fourth for the second part of the horseshoe. You get a lot of G-loading here. Out of the horseshoe, accelerating as you do so, and up to a sequence of chicanes. You have a right-left, and as soon as you are through this – at about 100 m.p.h. – you are presented with another left-hander. It's quite demanding, third gear. Accelerating through this corner at 80 to 90 m.p.h.

Then it's into a short curve rather than a straight, taking you back towards the pits. Up through the gears again. Third, fourth, fifth. You're upwards of 150 m.p.h. along this stretch of the circuit. Now down to fourth gear for a long left-hander, which you take at 120 to 130 m.p.h.

You are hanging on, determined to try to keep to the inside of the track. Holding, holding, holding. Then, at the last possible moment,

Below left: *Out of Virage du Pont – accelerating to the line*

Below right: *Times check with the Williams' crew, 1988*

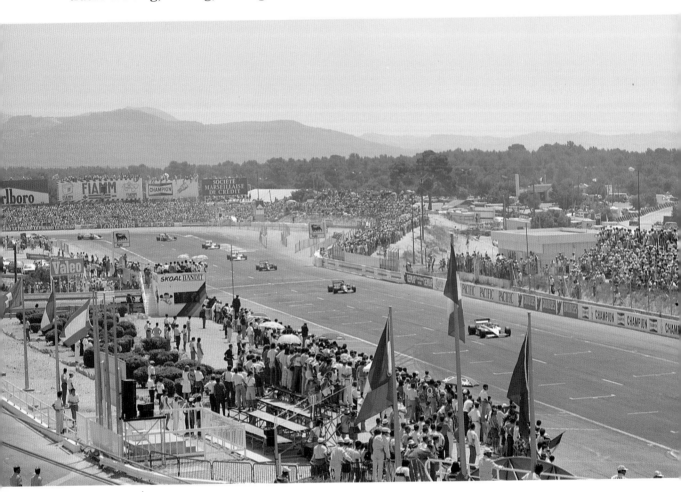

you are cutting across to hit the apex of the last corner, the right-hander to Virage du Pont.

This is a line you want to get right because you want to be as tight as you can coming out of the corner onto the pits straight. As I've said, depending on your ratios, it's a second-or third-gear corner. Accelerating up to the line. By the end of that straight you are up to 170 to 180 m.p.h. in sixth.

Le Castellet   Fact file

Circuit length: 2·369 miles, 3·813 km.
Race distance: 80 laps (189·543 miles, 305·04 km.)
Qualifying lap record: Nigel Mansell (Williams Honda) 1m. 6·454s., in 1987
Race lap record: Nelson Piquet (Williams Honda) 1m. 9·548s. at 122·641 m.p.h., in 1987

Winners: 1971, Jackie Stewart (Tyrrell Ford); 1973, Ronnie Peterson (Lotus Ford); 1975, Niki Lauda (Ferrari); 1976, James Hunt (McLaren Ford); 1978, Mario Andretti (Lotus Ford); 1980, Alan Jones (Williams Ford); 1982, René Arnoux (Renault); 1983, Alain Prost (Renault); 1985, Nelson Piquet (Brabham BMW); 1986, Nigel Mansell (Williams Honda); 1987, Nigel Mansell (Williams Honda); 1988, Alain Prost (McLaren Honda)

Nigel Mansell: 1982, did not enter (Lotus Ford); 1983, retired (Lotus Ford); 1985, did not start (Williams Honda); 1986, 1st (Williams Honda); 1987, 1st (Williams Honda); 1988, retired (Williams Judd)

8 BRITAIN

Circuit: *Silverstone*

Silverstone is not only Nigel Mansell's home circuit, it is the home of the World Championship itself. The first race of the first title season was held here on 13 May, 1950. It was won by Guiseppe Farina in an Alfa Romeo, the combination that went on to win the crown.

The circuit was created from the confusion and austerity of post-war Britain. There was an insatiable appetite for sport. Football grounds were bursting at the seams. But the motor racing circuits had either fallen into disrepair or were still being used by the forces. There were certainly no funds for a new purpose-built track, but the RAC Competition Committee saw the opportunity of utilizing a redundant airfield. Runways, perimeter roads and a little imagination would do the job.

The RAC discovered – as had, to the annoyance of the Constabulary, a few locals – that a former bomber base in the Midlands had ideal wide, flat runways to suit their purpose. A lease was granted and the RAC Grand Prix fixed for 2 October, 1948. The aerodrome was in Northamptonshire, near the village of Silverstone.

That first circuit took the cars along the runways to the intersection point, where they turned hard left. To put out of mind any prospect of a head-on with cars making a similar manoeuvre from the opposite direction, the organizers positioned, at the appropriate spot, canvas screens! Simple, really. Out of sight . . . The track was lined with straw bales and oil drums, the spectators stationed behind ropes. Basic scaffolding and tents created the pits and officials' quarters.

Be it ever so humble, there was no place like a new home for British motor racing. That first Grand Prix had them jamming the roads to Silverstone and then spilling onto the track in celebration at the end. (Some things don't really change that much at all.) The winner was Italian Luigi Villoresi, in a Maserati, at a speed of 72·2 m.p.h. What did change,

Above: *The airfield that launched the World Championship*

Left: *Silverstone circuit is born and Grand Prix racing is back on the road, 1948*

Right: *Guiseppe Farina on course for victory in the first World Championship race, 1950*

of course, was the lay-out and speeds. Alain Prost and Nigel Mansell, in recent seasons, won here at more than 146 m.p.h.

Silverstone staged the British Grand Prix in 1949, and the circuit took on the shape recognizable today. Gone were the converging runway sections. The full perimeter road was used with a low-gear chicane at Club. It was another Maserati victory, the driver a Swiss baron, Emmanuel de Graffenried.

The Club chicane was gone when Silverstone hosted the inaugural World Championship race. In recognition of the occasion it was called the Grand Prix d'Europe, though it became known as Royal Silverstone. King George VI and Queen Elizabeth looked on as Dr Farina led the Maserati one-two-three demonstration of superiority. His average speed, 90·96 m.p.h.

Through the years that followed the names of Silverstone corners and curves were to become as familiar as the names of the drivers. Becketts Corner and Chapel Curve derive from the Chapel of Thomas à Becket, the ruins of which lie nearby; Abbey Curve from Luffield Abbey; Stowe Corner from Stowe School; Maggotts Curve from Maggotts Moor; Copse Corner from Seven Copses Wood. Two aircraft hangars alongside the track inspired the naming of Hangar Straight. The RAC decided to name Club Corner after their Pall Mall club, and Woodcote Corner after their country club at Woodcote Park, in Surrey.

In 1975, a chicane was introduced at Woodcote Corner which had now become extremely fast and potentially lethal. But even with the chicane, many drivers feared a car could be launched into the crowd. Before it was changed again, for the 1987 British Grand Prix, Niki Lauda said: 'I would not want anyone who meant anything to me to be sitting over there'.

Mike Hawthorn . . . a chap of the '50s

The revised corner is taken in second gear, but has had little effect on the overall speed, and speed is the essence of Silverstone. It is sometimes dismissed as flat and boring. Certainly it doesn't have the tumbling terrain or natural amphitheatre of Brands Hatch, which was left out in the cold when the Northants track was given an exclusive five-year World Championship contract running from 1987. But it has speed, mind-blowing speed.

In qualifying for the 1985 British Grand Prix, Keke Rosberg confirmed Silverstone's status as the fastest of all Formula One tracks with a qualifying lap of more than 160 m.p.h. Even with the new Woodcote chicane and sixty-seven yards of extra track, Nigel Mansell and Nelson Piquet were close to that figure in 1987 qualifying.

In the early days of Silverstone, it wasn't only the pace that was gentler. There was none of the hype and intensity that come with the chopper and mega-buck age. Mike Hawthorn was very much a chap of the fifties. When he crossed the line in second place at the 1958 British Grand Prix, he required no persuading to take a pint of beer from the marshals.

By now the British round of the World Championship was alternating between Silverstone and Aintree. From the mid-sixties up to that exclusive contract, it would alternate with Brands Hatch. The straw bales and oil drums gave way to sturdier barriers as safety measures were improved. Two fatal accidents in the pits promoted the building of an elevated pit road. Wider run-off areas and the Woodcote chicane came with the next wave of changes.

By 1973, Woodcote Corner had become blindingly quick and in the Grand Prix that year Jody Scheckter lost control of his McLaren first time round, causing a massive pile-up. Nine cars were eliminated and, although no one was seriously hurt, the chicane was introduced for the 1975 race. There was also a new pits complex and the beginnings of what is still a growth area, hospitality suites. That 1975 Grand Prix also had its problems. This time the hazard was rain. Proceedings were halted when a dozen cars slithered and spun off the track.

Silverstone has been the scene of some great British triumphs: Peter Collins in 1958; Jim Clark in 1963, '65 and '67; Jackie Stewart in 1969 and '71; James Hunt in 1977; John Watson in 1981; and then, after that pulsating duel with Williams team-mate Nelson Piquet, Nigel Mansell in 1987.

Thousands spilled onto the circuit to share Mansell's joy; the man himself kissed the tarmac where he overtook the Brazilian. He was the people's hero again the following year, even if he couldn't deny Ayrton Senna another win in the all-conquering McLaren. He splashed through the puddles to claim a stirring second place with his first finish of the season.

Silverstone now has not only another Woodcote chicane, but also another pit complex, all part of a £1 million improvement programme. More development work is planned as the circuit that took off from a wartime airfield enters its fifth decade. The chances are that the years to come will prove just as eventful as those that have passed.

Harry Clow 89.

Nothing can lift a driver more than racing on home ground. No matter how long you have driven, how much experience you have had, how much success you've achieved, the magic of racing in your own country never fades. It is the most majestic feeling. You are out there competing, waving the flag, for Queen and country. If that doesn't stir you, there's something wrong with you.

What makes it particularly special, of course, is the response of the fans. Naturally they are going to get behind a British driver, but our fans are among the most knowledgeable in the world. They understand motor racing, they know exactly what's going on and they demonstrate their appreciation when it is appropriate. Those scenes at the end of the 1987 Grand Prix will stay with me forever. I'm grateful we were able to share that great day together because, believe me, the fans were very much a part of it.

The British fans were with me right from the start of my winning streak. My first victory was in the 1985 Grand Prix of Europe at Brands Hatch, and I followed it up with a win in the British Grand Prix at Brands the following year. That was tremendous enough, but then to come to Silverstone in 1987 and have a day like that was unbelievable. Even 1988 was fantastic because we'd had such a disappointing season and then got second place in the wet. I reckon three firsts and a second in four years is a record to be proud of.

I've made a habit of staying in a caravan at the circuit with my family and being part of the Silverstone scene. It's convenient, and the fans let me have my private time to relax and be with my family and friends. They are not only supportive but also respectful.

What gives Silverstone a character all of its own is its speed. When you consider that Nelson Piquet and I were racing each other – and

Above left: *Salute for the people's hero*

Above right: *. . . leading Piquet round the final corner, 1987*

Right: *Nigel savours his greatest victory, 1987*

I mean *racing* – at average speeds of more than 150 m.p.h., you realize just how fast this track is. And that, remember, is with the new, second-gear Woodcote chicane. A lot of the other corners are incredibly fast. You have to be very precise as to where you position the car.

Being a flat, open aerodrome circuit, Silverstone can present you with the problem of wind. There is none of the shelter you get at a woodland circuit like Brands Hatch. Unfortunately for the spectators they are able to see only one part of the circuit, but from a driver's point of view there's no way it can be boring when you are travelling at these speeds and having to be this accurate. It is a circuit with a lot of special qualities and features.

It's certainly not dull, I promise you. It is thrilling, challenging, exhilarating. It's also home, and as I've found, there's no place like it.

Lap of Silverstone

On a fast lap at Silverstone you come out of the Woodcote chicane, accelerating, second, third, fourth, fifth, and are already into sixth gear by the time you cross the start/finish line. You are probably doing 150 to 160 m.p.h. You actually enter Copse Corner, a right-hander, at 170 to 180 m.p.h., changing down to fourth, sometimes riding up to the outside of the kerb, at around 140 m.p.h. It's not too bad if it's dry. If it's wet, you don't touch any of the kerbs.

Through Copse, then up to fifth and sixth, flat out, for the sling-shot through Maggotts. Approaching Becketts at 175 to 180 m.p.h. Braking fairly hard, third or fourth gear, depending on your ratios. Using all the circuit here, trying to hit the apex on the other side and then drifting right out to the ripple strips on the outside. You're taking this corner at probably 120-plus m.p.h.

As soon as you start sliding out of Becketts, you're up into fifth and still in fifth, flat, taking Chapel. Just as you're exiting Chapel to go down Hangar Straight, you pull sixth. Down the straight it's flat-out sixth, approaching 200 m.p.h. Here is one of the good overtaking opportunities at Silverstone, and for me one overtaking manoeuvre in particular sticks in my mind.

This is the point where I caught Nelson in 1987. There were only a couple of laps left, but I'd been planning my move for probably ten laps before I executed it. He saw me coming in his mirrors. I was low on fuel, but I had to turn up the boost. I feinted to the left, then to the right, then a second time to the left. This time I made a more obvious movement with my car, actually taking it across the circuit.

As soon as Nelson saw this he was convinced I was going to overtake him on the outside. He moved his head on the left-hand mirror, and the car to the left. At that stage I was still in his slipstream at more than 200 m.p.h., and the rest was relatively easy.

I switched back to the right and just missed his gearbox as I dived for the inside. He tried to come back and we almost touched going into Stowe, but I was in front and away.

Nigel, in the Williams'
No. 5, begins his charge
through the spray

Normally Stowe is taken in fifth, but in qualifying in 1988 some of the cars went through there flat in sixth, or with virtually no lift, anyway. I tried it. It's incredibly quick and it's dangerous. Even on a racing lap, though, all you do is gently dab the brakes at the end of Hangar Straight, change down to fifth and then go through flat, at 160 m.p.h.

Up into sixth, if you're not there already, heading for another incredible corner at Club. How close the gearbox ratios are – and I've had mine quite close at Silverstone – will determine your selection here. I have found changing down to fifth gives me just a bit more traction. You don't touch the brakes, you just have what is known in the game as a 'confidence lift'. You make sure you get the apex, and then you're flat out, 160-plus m.p.h.

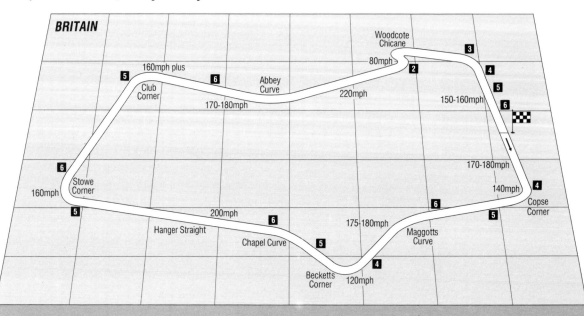

. . . to a glorious second place

Grab sixth, then up towards Abbey. This is a left-hand bend and there are a few bumps here. You take Abbey Curve absolutely flat, 170 to 180 m.p.h., depending on how much power you've got. Down towards Woodcote it's as quick if not quicker than Hangar Straight, depending on which way the wind is blowing.

A little extra care is needed here. Because I've driven at Silverstone for so many years I keep thinking of the fast chicane, and I'm ready in fourth when I realize it's all changed. Now it's second gear – and the road turns left, not right! You brake hard and take the chicane at 80 m.p.h. instead of 140 m.p.h. It's left-right, accelerating, wheel-spin coming out, second, third, fourth, fifth and sixth across the start/finish line again.

The reception I had when I crossed that line for the last time in 1987 gave me the best feeling I've ever had in my life. Whatever else I achieve in my career, the memory of that day will live with me forever.

Silverstone Fact file

Circuit length: 2·969 miles, 4·778 km.
Race distance: 65 laps (192·985 miles, 310·571 km.)
Qualifying lap record: Nelson Piquet (Williams Honda) 1m. 7·110s., in 1987
Race lap record: Nigel Mansell (Williams Honda) 1m. 9·832s. at 153·054 m.p.h., in 1987

Winners: 1950, Guiseppe Farina (Alfa Romeo); 1951, Froilan Gonzalez (Ferrari); 1952, Alberto Ascari (Ferrari); 1953, Alberto Ascari (Ferrari); 1954, Froilan Gonzalez (Ferrari); 1956, Juan-Manuel Fangio (Lancia-Ferrari); 1958, Peter Collins (Ferrari); 1960, Jack Brabham (Cooper Climax); 1963, Jim Clark (Lotus Climax); 1965, Jim Clark (Lotus Climax); 1967, Jim Clark (Lotus Ford); 1969, Jackie Stewart (Matra Ford); 1971, Jackie Stewart (Tyrrell Ford); 1973, Peter Revson (McLaren Ford); 1975, Emerson Fittipaldi (McLaren Ford); 1977, James Hunt (McLaren Ford); 1979, Clay Regazzoni (Williams Ford); 1981, John Watson (McLaren Ford); 1983, Alain Prost (Renault); 1985, Alain Prost (McLaren TAG); 1987, Nigel Mansell (Williams Honda); 1988, Ayrton Senna (McLaren Honda)

Nigel Mansell: 1981, did not qualify (Lotus Ford); 1983, 4th (Lotus Renault); 1985, retired (Williams Honda); 1987, 1st (Williams Honda); 1988, 2nd (Williams Judd)

9 GERMANY

Circuit: **Hockenheim**

The German Grand Prix has perhaps the most grisly record of all Formula One World Championship races: Argentina's Onofre Marimon was killed during practice in 1954; Britain's Peter Collins, killed in the race, 1958; Holland's Carel Godin de Beaufort, killed in practice, 1964; Britain's John Taylor, killed in the race, 1966; Germany's Gerhard Mitter, killed in practice, 1969.

Collins died at Avus, the others at the formidable Nürburgring. But it was another accident and near fatality which marked the end of the road for that old fourteen-mile circuit. Niki Lauda, the Austrian seemingly on course to retain his title in 1976, was hideously burnt when his Ferrari crashed and burst into flames.

Earlier that year Lauda, recognizing the extreme dangers of the Nürburgring, recommended a boycott of the race at a drivers' meeting, but was voted down. At the end of that season the circuit lost its FIA licence. Lauda says, 'I recall bits before the accident. I recall bits after. But I recollect nothing during, not a damn thing. Except a big black hole. Returning to the spot where it all took place stirs no emotions in me at all. Even if I go back fifty times, it will always leave me cold.'

The Grand Prix was switched to Hockenheim, a circuit already associated with one of the saddest losses to motor racing. It was here, in a Formula Two race, that Jim Clark was killed on 7 April 1968. He was there only because the car he should have been racing at Brands Hatch wasn't ready. It was an accident that made every other driver in the sport feel utterly vulnerable.

Hockenheim then had no chicanes and few guardrails. Situated fifteen miles southwest of the enchanting town of Heidelberg, it was originally a motor-cycling track, intended, no doubt, for those of split personality. It is really two circuits: the first heads out into the pine forest, along a long straight, turns at the Ost Kurve, and returns by means of another long straight; the second is the double loop contained within the stadium of huge concrete stands.

As speeds and fears increased, the two long straights were broken up by chicanes. A third chicane was introduced at the daunting Ost Kurve after yet another fatal accident in 1980. Frenchman Patrick Depailler was killed here during testing.

The morbid catalogue continued in 1982 when Ferrari's Didier Pironi, looking good for victory that weekend and in the Championship itself, was badly injured during a rainswept Saturday morning practice session. The weather can change rapidly at Hockenheim. Hot sunshine often gives way to rainstorms, and here that is perilous. Spray is suspended between the trees like a massive blanket, obscuring vision and testing the nerve of the bravest.

Niki Lauda on the day of his horrendous crash at the old Nürburgring, 1976

Hockenheim actually made its Grand Prix debut in 1970, one of only two excursions from the Nürburgring before 1977. That first race here was won by the Austrian Jochen Rindt. It was his last win. He was killed a month later at Monza, and is recorded as the only posthumous World Champion. The sombre connections are somehow in keeping with a circuit that isn't renowned for firing the imagination or raising expectations. There is usually so little in the atmosphere and the racing to set the pulse racing.

There were, at least, a few laughs during the race of 1982. Nelson Piquet and Eliseo Salazar tangled at a chicane and both spun out of the contest. Piquet, incensed, confronted the Chilean at the side of the track. The Brazilian, not content with trading verbal blows, then proceeded to aim kicks and punches. Not, it should be said, with a great deal of effect. As a bemused Salazar pointed out: 'He kept screaming and hitting me on the head, but I was still wearing my helmet. I didn't feel a thing.' All around the globe the media gobbled it up.

Above: *The track loops beneath the stands of Hockenheim's stadium*

Left: *Out into the forest, Nigel Mansell and the Williams Judd, 1988*

Austrian Gerhard Berger wasn't too amused when, in 1987, person or persons unknown made off with the wing of his Ferrari after he crashed during practice. Broadcast appeals for its return proved fruitless, so a replacement had to be sent up from Maranello in time for business the following day.

The new Nürburgring was given the 1985 German Grand Prix (after staging the 1984 Grand Prix of Europe), but Hockenheim has since been confirmed as the home of the race. If it remains so for long enough, maybe it will earn a little more affection.

Nigel Mansell has not found it the happiest of hunting grounds. His best result is third, which he managed in 1986 after the two McLarens ran out of fuel. Prospects looked brighter the following year, when he seemed guaranteed second place at least. He and Alain Prost were in a race of their own. Both, alas, were forced to retire and Nelson Piquet inherited a win that was to prove crucial to the outcome of the World Championship.

H OCKENHEIM is one of those circuits – Monaco is another – where I feel I must have a change of luck and some good races waiting for me. I've by no means had the best of fortune so far. Even in my Formula Two days it was the same. I was winning an F2 race but had problems towards the end and came second instead. Yes, I'd say I'm owed a victory here.

I wouldn't criticize the reasoning behind the chicanes here. The straights were obviously very long and very fast. The Ost Kurve was also extremely fast. I just feel, though, that the way they have changed the circuit has not done anything for the character of the place. I think it would have been better to move back the barriers and have a lot of sand-traps. That way you would still have adequate safety measures but more interesting, challenging corners.

I stress, though, that I do not wish to be overcritical because the changes were made with good intent and, regardless of personal feelings or experience, you have to go in there with a positive, optimistic attitude. It's another Championship race, another nine points are at stake. Once you're here, you get on with the job.

With those long straights it is still, overall, a very fast circuit, but it's one of those places where you have to compromise when you set up the car. You don't want too much drag along these straights if you are to reach competitive top speeds, and yet you need enough download for the infield section. You want to be quick through here and the chicanes, and not destroy your tyres in the process.

It is a circuit that can take a heavy toll on machinery. You are on full throttle for long periods of time, getting out of it every ounce you can; then you are braking very heavily, going down through the gearbox, and, as you accelerate hard, it's back up again. It's not really surprising you get quite a lot of retirements here.

On the driver it is not particularly hard, not compared with some circuits. But when it rains here you can have serious problems. When it's wet, this is one of the most dangerous circuits in the world. It is a long circuit – more than four miles – and a lot of the track is out in the forest. Tall trees either side give it a tunnel effect.

The cars throw rainwater thirty to forty feet into the air, and because of the trees it cannot be dispersed. It is bad enough trying to cope with the usual spray, but then when you get this vapour mist, this fogging effect, you really cannot see a thing. It is very dangerous, and very unsettling for the driver.

Chicanes have checked Hockenheim's speeds

Lap of Hockenheim

You are coming out of the stadium, along the start/finish straight, and in sixth gear heading for a very fast right-hander. You take it in fourth gear, doing probably 130 m.p.h. Then it's up to fifth and sixth as you set out on one of these long straights. It's simply full throttle, flat out, pedalling as fast as your car and your engine will go. Getting up to a genuine 200 m.p.h. here.

After this long blast you have to brake very, very hard, probably at about the 100- to 150-metre board, depending on track conditions, and you are down into second gear. It's slow, it's very tight. It's tight right, tight left. You can't hit the kerbs – or at least you don't want to – because they are very high here.

There's not much traction to help you coming out of here, but you are accelerating as quickly as you can and up through the gears: second, third, fourth, fifth, sixth. Down another straight. In fact it is more of a curve to the right. Not quite as long as the previous straight, but still fast. Upwards of 180 m.p.h.

Again, at the end of the straight you are braking hard, but instead of a second-gear chicane, the Ost Kurve is third gear because you

can bounce across the kerbs a bit here. It's not recommended to bounce too hard, though. If you do that you could find yourself flying off the circuit on the outside. The Ost Kurve was, and to a certain extent still is, a great corner. The chicane is a little before it and you get a lot of G-loading going through the corner, and coming out of it.

Through this curve, exiting in fifth, then up to sixth gear for the back straight. Another fast stretch, pushing hard. Ahead now is Chicane Two (as distinct from the Ost Kurve chicane), which is much, much faster than the first chicane. Instead of 40 to 50 m.p.h., you are talking about 120 to 130 m.p.h. It's a fourth gear, switchback chicane. To the left, to the right, then left again. You don't want to touch the kerbs going in, but about halfway through you do tend to slide up the kerbs. Also when you are coming out.

Back onto the straight again, fifth, sixth gear, heading for the stadium. As you approach Agip Kurve, you are probably doing about 190 m.p.h. Agip Kurve is the right-hander which brings you into the stadium itself. This is the bumpiest part of the circuit, because a tunnel goes underneath the track at this point. It has been resurfaced many times, but it always subsides and gives you a bumpy entrance to the stadium. For this right-hander you are down to fourth gear.

Now you are along a short straight, in front of the stands, and up into fifth. Then you are braking very hard at the Sachs Kurve, which is a left-hand hairpin. Overtaking opportunity here and good viewing,

Above: *'When it's wet, Hockenheim is one of the most dangerous circuits in the world'*

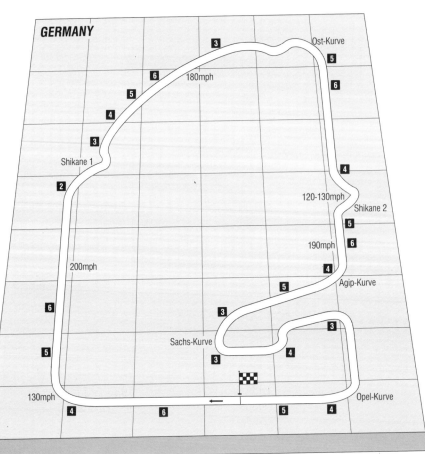

of course, for the people in the stadium. Sachs Kurve is second or third gear. This hairpin and Chicane One are the slowest parts of the circuit.

Out of Sachs Kurve, accelerating up to fourth gear through a left-hander. Then it's a right-hander going into Opel Kurve. This is the last corner and very important for your momentum towards the line and the straight. You change down to third gear, accelerate through, then change back up through the gears, fourth, fifth and sixth as you complete the lap.

Hockenheim Fact file

Circuit length: 4·223 miles, 6·797 km.
Race distance: 44 laps (185·832 miles, 299·068 km.)
Qualifying lap record: Keke Rosberg (McLaren TAG) 1m. 42·013s., in 1986
Race lap record: Nigel Mansell (Williams Honda) 1m. 45·716s. at 143·826 m.p.h., in 1987

Winners: 1970, Jochen Rindt (Lotus Ford); 1977, Niki Lauda (Ferrari); 1978, Mario Andretti (Lotus Ford); 1979, Alan Jones (Williams Ford); 1980, Jacques Laffite (Ligier Ford); 1981, Nelson Piquet (Brabham Ford); 1982, Patrick Tambay (Ferrari); 1983, René Arnoux (Ferrari); 1984, Alain Prost (McLaren TAG); 1986, Nelson Piquet (Williams Honda); 1987, Nelson Piquet (Williams Honda); 1988, Ayrton Senna (McLaren Honda)

Nigel Mansell: 1981, retired (Lotus Ford); 1982, 9th (Lotus Ford); 1983, retired (Lotus Renault); 1984, 4th (Lotus Renault); 1986, 3rd (Williams Honda); 1987, retired (Williams Honda); 1988, accident (Williams Judd)

10 HUNGARY

Circuit: Budapest (Hungaroring)

Formula One is constantly seeking new frontiers, dedicated to the mission of enhancing its reputation as the genuine World Championship. For some years there had been talk of taking the show behind the Iron Curtain, even to the streets of Moscow. That particular venture remains no more than an intriguing thought, but on 10 September 1985, FISA signed the agreement that put Eastern Europe on the Grand Prix map.

The site for this historic event was found on barren, rolling land, near the village of Mogyorod. Barely twelve miles away was the centre of Budapest, and the Hungarian capital opened its arms to the multi-million pound business called Formula One motor racing.

But before they could get their hands on all that foreign currency, they had work to do back at the site. The new track would take advantage of the natural contours and meet all modern specifications and safety standards. Construction work, which would cost £3 million, started on 15 October 1985. It was finished in time for the first trial race, on 13 June 1986. On 10 August 1986, the World Championship was welcomed to the Hungaroring.

Formula One's travelling band – at best dubious about the whole thing – were pleasantly surprised. Organization and facilities were excellent, enthusiasm boundless. Good hotels, along the banks of the Danube, were just twenty minutes away. A motorway link made the journey simple, even if the traffic police were apt to be a little overzealous.

The circuit itself was found to be undulating – the difference between the highest and lowest points is 34·5 metres – and slow: one straight followed by a series of corners and bends. The track had to bend even more than was originally planned to avoid a previously unknown spring.

It meant that overtaking opportunities would be limited, so a good grid position would be particularly important. Another problem was the dust, which reduced grip and made 'the line' an even more precious piece of tarmac. Venture too far off it and you could be spinning right out of the action.

But action there was, and the Hungarian Grand Prix was declared a success. Scorching sunshine greeted that first Formula One weekend here, and spectators in shorts and colourful sponsors' hats filled the great banks in their scores of thousands. As the locals pointed out, they did, after all, have a proud motor racing tradition. The first generally acknowledged Grand Prix, held at Le Mans in 1906, was won by a Hungarian, Ferenc Szisz. Hungary also staged a race in 1956.

Racing enthusiasts – or merely the curious – also came in from Czechoslovakia, East Germany and Rumania. Many travelled from the West. Vienna is, after all, only 160 miles away. Over the first three years of the event, the number of visitors more than doubled. Budapest hotels

Hungaroring . . . undulating, twisting, demanding

were fully booked five months before the 1988 race. The organizers brought into their net accommodation in the outlying districts. They say they can now cope with the demands of 50,000 visitors. Grand Prix weekend has fallen on Budapest like manna from heaven.

When the sound of gipsy violins gives way to the grunt of Grand Prix racing cars, it makes no difference whether it's East or West. Time for work and the familiar objective. Once inside the paddock gates, the Formula One band are in their own little world, cloistered from any conflict of political ideals and social restraints.

At that first Formula One working weekend at the Hungaroring, Nigel

Mansell announced the completion of negotiations for a new two-year contract with Williams, celebrated his birthday and was fastest in the opening qualifying session. But after the second session he was fourth, and in the race had to settle for third place behind his Williams team-mate Nelson Piquet – who had made a decisive adjustment to his differential – and Ayrton Senna in the Lotus.

Twelve months later there was another contractual announcement. Piquet would be switching to Lotus at the end of the season (Senna was bound for McLaren), and Mansell sensed then that because Piquet would be retaining a Honda connection his own Championship prospects were dim. Not that he allowed his suspicions to affect his performance on the track.

He took pole with one of the outstanding laps of his career. Watching

The fans came in their scores of thousands . . .

from the back of the paddock that day was Benetton team boss, Peter Collins. He said: 'People go on about Nigel's courage and determination, but that lap wasn't just about courage and determination. It was skill and precision driving. It was brilliant.'

He was equally dominant in the race, cruising to what seemed inevitable victory. But then, with just over five laps – thirteen miles – to go, a wheel-retaining nut came off his right rear. The wheel tilted and the car snaked to a halt. He wasn't able even to drive it back to the pits. Piquet was presented with another win.

In 1988 Nigel turned up at the Hungaroring suffering from the effects of chicken pox. Still he qualified second in the Judd-powered Williams, and put up a bold fight in the race. Ultimately, though, he had to give in to exhaustion and retired. This time victory was Senna's.

ON reflection I suppose I shouldn't have raced that weekend. I'd lost a lot of weight and strength through my illness. In fact, it took me some time to fully recover and I had to miss the following two races. But then it's always easier to be wise after the event. At the time I didn't want to let anyone down and felt I should race. I was doing all right, running second. But as I got weaker I had a spin, dropped down to fourth and eventually retired myself.

This is a demanding circuit at the best of times. You really do need your fitness here. It's one corner after another, all go all the time. You have no time to rest. In fact you've almost no time to breathe. It's just work, work, work. As it's a slow circuit it's a long race in terms of time, so that by the end you can be drained physically.

It is such a tight, twisting circuit that overtaking is very difficult indeed. Your best chance – often your only chance – is at the end of the start/finish straight. You have got to be very precise here because there is only one line. Move off it, even just a little, and you'll probably find yourself falling off the circuit.

But it is an interesting circuit, well laid out with lots of good viewing positions for the fans. And there have been plenty of fans to see the races. The support and response has been tremendous. It's heartening to see such phenomenal crowds.

I suppose we weren't really sure what to expect when we went into

. . . as Grand Prix racing went behind the Iron Curtain

Eastern Europe for the first time, but they've done an incredibly professional job. A lot of time, effort and money have been spent presenting a circuit which is just about first class. The facilities are very good, and the track itself is good from a driver's point of view. It's difficult to get the job done, but that is all part of the challenge of a racing track.

It's one of those circuits where things haven't quite worked out for me yet. I was very close in 1987, leading with no worries at all until that wheelnut fell off. So I would like to think it owes me one in the not too distant future.

Lap of Budapest

This is one of the slowest circuits in Grand Prix racing, with average speeds of around 95 to 99 m.p.h., because the only straight is in front of the pits. It's about 700 metres long, so that if you have the power this is where you have got to try and take advantage of it. This, of course, is where the turbos had the upper hand. Through the slow corners it was a different matter.

So coming out of the final corner, down the straight and across the start/finish line, you're changing from fourth to fifth to sixth, for the

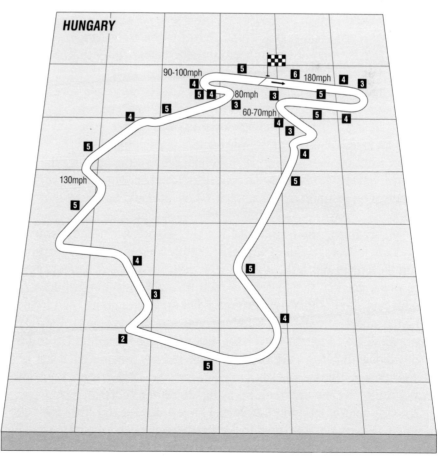

fastest part of the circuit. By the end of this straight you can be doing more than 180 m.p.h.

Mansell sets the pace in 1986 . . .

Then you are changing down to third for the right-hander. Coming out and accelerating down a short straight, changing up to fourth gear and then up to fifth. You are not in fifth for long, though. You're braking and changing back down to third gear to go round a very tight left-hander. Your speed here is only about 60 to 70 m.p.h.

Now sliding out and heading down another short straight. You're up to fourth and soon down to third again. This is typical of the circuit. Always working, never getting the chance to settle. And all the time you are having to take great care to stay on line. One lapse in concentration or effort could be all it takes. It could be the end of your race.

Down to third, then, and into a tight, complex chicane. Now it's right, now left, now sliding out for a slightly longer straight. Here you go up to fourth and fifth, holding it in fifth for the left-hander. It's a very quick corner. If you set yourself up right you don't brake. You just lift and then go flat out through, sliding, taking up all the circuit.

Just a short straight here before you are braking quite hard and changing down to fourth for a long, sweeping right-hander. Up to fifth again, along that top part of the circuit before braking hard for one of the slower chicanes here. Down to second gear, right, then left, through the chicane and then up again, third and fourth.

You are quickly into another corner, a left-hander, but this you take in fourth. Staying in fourth as the track sweeps round to the right. As soon as you come out of this one, you're up into fifth gear. Flat out

. . . but in 1988 it's Senna

round a quick left, and then a quick right. Keeping it in fifth until you come to another right-hander. Those fifth-gear corners are taken at about 130 m.p.h. Another section where you have to be very precise, very careful.

At this right-hander you are braking quite hard, changing down to fourth and flicking through the corner. Down a short straight now, and changing to fifth. Then you're braking hard again, and down into third for a long loop round to the left. You're taking this at around 80 m.p.h.

Coming out of the loop you're into a short straight and up through the gears, third, fourth, fifth, but soon back down to fourth again for the final corner on the circuit, a right-hander. Here you try to keep it as tight as possible. You're probably doing 90 to 100 m.p.h. Coming off the right-hander you are accelerating and going through the box again as you head down the start/finish straight.

Budapest Fact file

Circuit length: 2·494 miles, 4·013 km.
Race distance: 76 laps (189·558 miles, 305·064 km.)
Qualifying lap record: Ayrton Senna (McLaren Honda) 1m. 27·635s., in 1988
Race lap record: Nelson Piquet (Williams Honda) 1m. 30·149s. at 99·603 m.p.h., in 1987

Winners: 1986, Nelson Piquet (Williams Honda); 1987, Nelson Piquet (Williams Honda); 1988, Ayrton Senna (McLaren Honda)

Nigel Mansell: 1986, 3rd (Williams Honda); 1987, retired (Williams Honda); 1988, retired (Williams Judd)

11 BELGIUM

Circuit: **Spa-Francorchamps**

Ballot the drivers on their favourite circuit and the chances are the majority vote will go to the home of the Belgian Grand Prix. Sliced through the hills and forests of the Ardennes, it combines scenic splendour with one of the supreme racing challenges. It's fast and furious, yet has a distinctive 'Bus Stop' chicane and a genuine hairpin. It climbs and falls, sweeps and bends.

They've been racing in these parts since the twenties, and Spa-Francorchamps appears on the original list of the World Championship venues. It hosted a Grand Prix in all but a couple of the seasons up to 1970. The circuit then was 8·75 miles long, using public roads that took the cars out to Stavelot before hauling them back towards Francorchamps village. It was quick, extremely quick, and became an inevitable victim of the campaign for safer tracks.

The old circuit presented the first appearance of a woman in a Championship Grand Prix. Italian Maria de Filippis, driving a Maserati, finished tenth in the 1958 race. In 1966, Jackie Stewart went off and was trapped upside down in his car, petrol spilling over him. His BRM team-mate, Graham Hill, forfeited any chance of winning to stop and help release him.

Spa was the scene of the only Eagle-Weslake victory (Dan Gurney, 1967) and a momentous occasion in the McLaren story. Bruce McLaren steered his own car to the marque's first success in 1968. It proved to be the New Zealander's last, but the more recent achievements of the team serve as a fitting memorial.

Nivelles-Baulers twice held the Belgian race when the old Spa-Francorchamps was dropped, but from the mid-seventies until the early eighties it found a home at Zolder. It was not, however, a happy home. Two of the final Grand Prix weekends there were ravaged by controversy and tragedy.

During practice in 1981, the Argentine Carlos Reutemann, who drove for Williams, accidentally ran over Osella mechanic Giovanni Amadeo in the congested pit lane. He died the day after the race. At the start of the race itself Riccardo Patrese's Arrows stalled, and as mechanic Dave Luckett tried to get the Italian away Siegfried Stohr, in the other Arrows, ploughed into him. Amazingly, Luckett was not killed. Protesting drivers forced a halt to proceedings after two laps, and the eventual contest was hurriedly cut short when rain poured on the anguish for the harrassed organizers.

The one lighter incident that year was provided by French driver René Arnoux – then partner to Alain Prost at Renault – and a marshal dedicated to the task of order and control. Arnoux, unimpressed at the prospect of being trapped in a traffic jam as he left the circuit after

The way it was . . . Bruce McLaren's historic win at Spa, 1968

practice, attempted an alternative exit. The trusty marshal was having none of that and blocked Arnoux's path.

But Arnoux was equally insistent that he was not going to be stopped, whereupon the marshal gallantly threw himself onto the bonnet of the Renault 5. Still unmoved, Arnoux drove the three miles to his hotel with the poor marshal still on his bonnet. The police were called, and Arnoux was locked up to ponder the error of his way from the circuit.

The following year Zolder claimed the life of Gilles Villeneuve. His fatal accident on the Saturday plunged Zolder into an unbearable state of depression. One distinguished voice spoke for most with the conclusion: 'The only good thing about Zolder is the frites and mayonnaise'.

In 1983 the frites were still good, but now they were being served at Spa, and although the race was at Zolder in 1984 it made a permanent return to the Ardennes in 1985. It wasn't only the frites the Formula One band found to their liking in this corner of the country, close to the German border, thirty miles from Liège and Aachen. The circuit had been shortened by half yet had retained its awesome character.

The great tour up to Stavelot had been taken out and the public roads joined by a new section, from Les Combes to the replacement Stavelot Corner. The fork from La Source is normally open to traffic, but police don't take too kindly to enthusiasts plunging down the linking, purpose-built stretch to log a full lap.

During Grand Prix weekend the woods and fields are a patchwork quilt of tents. The less adventurous find accommodation in the small towns and villages that dot the hills and valleys. Spa itself, just a few minutes' drive over the brow from Francorchamps, boasts one of the best restaurants in the region. Excellent cuisine is not uncommon in this often understated country. As for Belgian chocolate, it's quite simply incomparable.

The dampener to this image of paradise can be, and frequently is, the weather. Just like the rest of us, rain clouds are attracted to the Ardennes, clinging to the hills and turning the job of driving a racing car into a lottery. This is still the longest circuit in terms of distance and lap

Nigel Mansell and the JPS Lotus, Zolder, 1982

times, and conditions can change from one part of the track to another.

The erratic nature of the weather here was illustrated in 1985, when the Grand Prix was scheduled for the beginning of June. In anticipation of the worst, the track had been resurfaced with a specially porous material. Instead the sun shone. Fiercely. So fiercely, in fact, that the track melted and the race was postponed.

It was given a new slot in mid-September, the track stayed in one piece and Nigel Mansell took a significant step in his career. He claimed second place, his best result to date. He immediately followed it up with his maiden victory in the Grand Prix of Europe at Brands Hatch. The momentum was maintained with another success in the next race, the South African Grand Prix at Kyalami.

When he returned to Spa in late May, 1986, he was again in search of a lift. He registered his first win of the season, and was launched into that thrilling assault on the Championship. The man he led home that day was the man he trailed the previous September, Ayrton Senna. They were again out in front in 1987 before their infamous tangles both on the circuit and in the pits. Alain Prost was able to go through and equal Jackie Stewart's all-time record of twenty-seven Grand Prix wins.

In 1988 Nigel was forced to withdraw from the Belgian race because of the effects of chicken pox. He also missed the Italian Grand Prix, returning to action in Portugal.

Scenic splendour,
supreme racing challenge

No doubt about it, this is one of the great circuits of the world. The setting is beautiful; the track is one for the purist driver. It's long, it climbs, it descends. It's fast, it's challenging and, in places, it's dangerous. It's the sort of circuit that makes a driver want to go out there and race. He knows it will test him and test his opponents. Marvellous place.

The whole weekend is good and stimulating. Pleasant area, good golf course nearby and, of course, it's the closest circuit to home. It's a quick hop in and out of Liège. In fact, for those with very light aircraft or helicopters, there's an air strip just up the road from the track, between Francorchamps and Spa.

Once you are out on the circuit there's no danger of the scenery becoming a distraction. You may notice something unusual or pick out certain things as you're going round. You may see someone reading a book at the side of the track. Even at high speed, things can seem to be in slow motion. It's really quite strange. But in reality, of course, the sighting is gone in an instant.

La Source . . .
whichever way you look
at it, a true hairpin

You certainly don't start looking sideways or allow your mind to wander. You don't think to yourself, what will I be doing in the morning? Or I wonder what I'll have for breakfast? Concentration is vital. You are always thinking about the job: how the track is, how the car is, how the race is going, what your strategy is going to be. Take your mind off the job and you are heading for trouble, that's for sure.

Any Grand Prix circuit has plenty to keep your mind occupied and Spa is no exception. It's not as fast as Silverstone, but it's still very quick. It's demanding and one of those circuits that require a bit of a compromise on aerodynamics because it has some chicanes, some medium-speed corners and some very fast corners, so you need enough wing on the car. You want to be competitive, but you want to be safe. If you're not safe on the very fast corners you're talking about a big off.

The weather can be such a crucial factor here. It frequently rains, and rain in itself can be bad enough. The dangerous complication arises when it's not raining all the way round the circuit. It quite often

happens that you're in sunshine by the pits area, and then in a downpour up in the hills at the far side of the circuit. It makes life very difficult and tyre choice critical. Any driver would tell you he'd prefer it wet or dry to wet and dry. In a situation like that luck plays too big a part. That's what we had to contend with in the race a couple of years ago. We just had to go with dry settings.

For all that it's a circuit I like immensely and I've had a couple of good results here. I had a second place in 1985, which I followed up with wins at Brands and Kyalami. Then I won here in 1986. In 1987 I was on pole. I made a tremendous start and built up a lead, but the race was stopped because of a big accident involving the two Tyrrells. The drivers, Jonathan Palmer and Philippe Streiff, were very fortunate to be unhurt.

Ayrton Senna managed to push his way through from the restart, but I was in good shape and going for the lead when we had that altercation. The incident on the track and the subsequent confrontation in the Lotus garage have been well chronicled. In 1988 I was too ill to race here, so I'm looking forward to competing in the Belgian Grand Prix again and hopefully getting back on the podium.

Lap of Spa-Francorchamps

You come onto the short pit straight from the 'Bus Stop' chicane, having snatched fourth gear and then gone up to fifth. Ahead is La Source, the hairpin, and from the actual start it's always tricky because everyone accelerates to be first in there. There's inevitably a lot of confusion, and instances of cars coming together are not unusual.

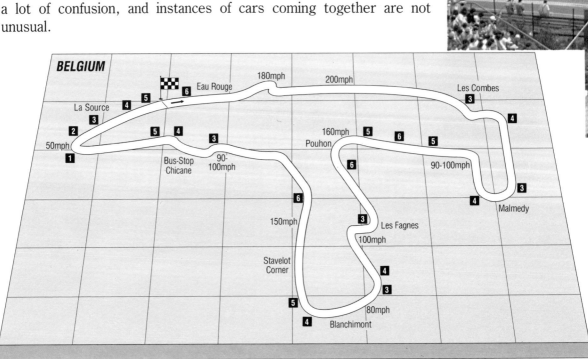

BELGIUM

Sweeping out of Eau Rouge . . . 'spectacular for the fans, potentially dangerous for the driver'

Along that pit straight you come very close to the barrier, and then swing across to the left-hand side of the circuit to get into the correct position for La Source. It is a true hairpin, so you have to slow right down, hard on the brakes. It's second gear, often first. It is very tight, a very important part of the circuit. You are taking it at about 50 m.p.h.

Round La Source and then down the hill, passing the old pits as you go up through the gears, second, third, fourth, fifth, sixth. Coming up now, one of the most sensational sections of track anywhere in Formula One. You are flat in sixth, still descending until you come into the dip at Eau Rouge. It's just a slight left, then right as you

sweep up the hill. It's spectacular for the fans, thrilling but potentially dangerous for the driver.

On a quick lap, even on reasonably full tanks if the car is set up right, you go up there flat out at about 180 m.p.h. – and you're entering a corner. You bottom out, the car goes very heavy and then it jumps up the hill. As it gets to the top it goes very light. If you are too far over to the left it can actually jump off the ground because there's quite a camber change at the top. The good line is on the right. The car goes light and just slides to the outside.

From there you come out onto the main straight. Along here, up towards Les Combes, you can easily reach up to 200 m.p.h. or more. Into Les Combes you change down, braking fairly hard, from sixth to third gear. Through the chicane, right-left-right, then snatch fourth for a short straight.

This takes you down to another right-hander, a 180-degree corner, at Malmedy. Third gear, fairly slow. Down towards a left-hand corner, which is about half the radius of Malmedy. Round this corner in fourth at about 90 to 100 m.p.h.

Rain turns the job of driving racing cars into a lottery

Now it's quite phenomenal because you are descending from the high point of the circuit. Downhill, the car accelerates very quickly. Fourth, fifth, sixth, approaching an incredible left-hander, which is Pouhon. Changing down to fifth gear, braking just slightly, and then as soon as you get into the corner you are flat out. You're taking this corner probably in excess of 160 m.p.h. It's very, very quick and you are actually changing up again during the exit.

Down the short straight to a right-left chicane, which is third or possibly fourth gear. Quite quick, about 100 m.p.h. Out of Les Fagnes, down another bit of straight to Blanchimont, an important third gear, right-hand corner which you take at around 80 m.p.h. There's a dip in the circuit just after the corner and coming up is Stavelot Corner. You need to get it right. Third, to fourth, to fifth and absolutely flat out through the Stavelot right-hander. Probably 150 m.p.h. through here, three or four lateral G-force.

Then it's flat out in sixth all the way down a straight, which in fact bends quite a bit, to the 'Bus Stop' chicane. Very panoramic here, but you don't really have time to appreciate the view. You are braking very hard for the chicane which is a one-off design, very much Spa's own. As the nickname suggests, you pull in like a bus to its stop.

The difference, of course, is that in a Formula One car you've no intention of stopping. You're going through in third gear at 90 to 100 m.p.h. It's left, right, right, left. The kerbs are too high to jump, yet if you do get a wheel on it will be accepted. Get two wheels on, though, and you're bouncing too much. They've done it well.

Coming out of the 'Bus Stop' you're thrown straight out towards the pit-lane. You are grabbing fourth gear as you exit and accelerate up through fifth, along the pit straight again. It's a long, testing lap, but it's exhilarating and a pleasure for anyone who likes real driving.

Spa-Francorchamps Fact file

Circuit length: 4·312 miles, 6·940 km.
Race distance: 43 laps (185·429 miles, 298·420 km.)
Qualifying lap record: Nigel Mansell (Williams Honda) 1m. 52·026s., in 1987
Race lap record: Alain Prost (McLaren TAG) 1m. 57·153s. at 132·513 m.p.h., in 1987

Winners: Old circuit – 1950, Juan-Manuel Fangio (Alfa Romeo); 1951, Guiseppe Farina (Alfa Romeo); 1952, Alberto Ascari (Ferrari); 1953, Alberto Ascari (Ferrari); 1954, Juan-Manuel Fangio (Maserati); 1955, Juan-Manuel Fangio (Mercedes-Benz); 1956, Peter Collins (Lancia-Ferrari); 1958, Tony Brooks (Vanwall); 1960, Jack Brabham (Cooper-Climax); 1961, Phil Hill (Ferrari); 1962, Jim Clark (Lotus Climax); 1963, Jim Clark (Lotus Climax); 1964, Jim Clark (Lotus Climax); 1965, Jim Clark (Lotus Climax); 1966, John Surtees (Ferrari); 1967, Dan Gurney (Eagle-Weslake); 1968, Bruce McLaren (McLaren Ford); 1970, Pedro Rodriguez (BRM). New circuit – 1983, Alain Prost (Renault); 1985, Ayrton Senna (Lotus Renault); 1986, Nigel Mansell (Williams Honda); 1987, Alain Prost (McLaren TAG); 1988, Ayrton Senna (McLaren Honda)

Nigel Mansell: 1983, retired (Lotus Ford); 1985, 2nd (Williams Honda); 1986, 1st (Williams Honda); 1987, retired (Williams Honda); 1988, did not enter (Williams Judd)

12 ITALY

Circuit: **Monza** *(Autodromo Nazionale)*

When you talk about passion and atmosphere in sport, your currency is devalued unless you have experienced Monza on the occasion of the Italian Grand Prix. The tranquil setting – a vast royal park ten miles north of Milan, with regal trees, acres of meadowland and endless lanes – scarcely prepares the first-time visitor. Awaiting the unsuspecting is an arena of emotion and ritual certainly unparalleled in Formula One motor racing.

That does not necessarily make Monza the most popular of venues. Here, unlike Imola, the exuberance can turn to hostility. In 1983 Alain Prost, locked in Championship combat with Nelson Piquet, a man who openly courted Italian affection, arrived here flanked by bodyguards. Another year he was pelted with stones and cans. He also revealed that during a test, straw was laid on the track in a deliberate attempt to throw him off. 'They are crazy, they do anything,' said the Frenchman.

Security guards with dogs patrol the paddock, the inner sanctum

Berger and Alboreto make it a day of celebrations for Ferrari

bordered with a high metal fence and a wall of faces. Even before the start of the race, teams are dismantling their canvas garages and packing their equipment. They've been here too often to be caught out again. At the end of the race Monza is bedlam. The guards and their dogs have evaporated; the mob take over.

The moment the winner crosses the line the invasion begins. They pour onto the track in their thousands, cars braking to avert carnage. They swarm down the straight to the podium; they scurry towards the pits and paddock, seeking out souvenirs, bits of broken wing, old tyres, anything; or simply they yearn to tell Papa: 'I stood close to the Ferrari.'

Ferrari, of course, is the great god at this shrine. Out in the park, through the stands, up in the trees and clinging to advertising hoardings, they are swathed in Ferrari favours. The most faithful, however, cannot have anticipated Ayrton Senna's demise and the one-two for the scarlet cars of Gerhard Berger and Michele Alboreto in 1988. It was the only

. . . and for their adoring fans in 1988

race of the season not won by McLaren. The scenes, even by Monza   *Last respects*
standards, were extraordinary. And all this just a month after the death
of the Old Man himself, Enzo Ferrari.

Whatever else you care to say about this place and these people, you
cannot dispute that motor racing *means* something here. Like any
modern sporting event of stature, it has its share of hospitality enclosures
and free-loaders. But Monza remains essentially the people's racetrack;
decaying and frayed at the edges; yet earthy, solid and committed.

It is, of course, rich in tradition. Italy and Britain are the only nations
to have staged a Grand Prix every year since the World Championship
began. (France missed out in 1955.) Monza itself has hosted all the
Italian races except that of 1980, which went to Imola. The archaic
stands and the crumbling bankings of the old oval circuit are reminders
of Monza's heritage. All about, you sense the spirits of great racing
drivers past.

For too long here the teams have had to contend with inadequate
facilities and dangerously cramped conditions in the pits, a situation
made all the more ludicrous by the enormous expanse of track along
the start/finish straight. But then Monza, like Monaco, is a special case.
How could you have a Grand Prix motor racing World Championship
without Monza?

The history of Grand Prix racing here goes back to 1922. Pietro
Bordini led the way that day, driving a two-litre Fiat 804. Wartime tanks
left their marks on the circuit, but it was restored to acceptable condition
for the 1949 race, won by Alberto Ascari in a Ferrari. Another Italian,

Peter Gethin's historic victory, 1971

Guiseppe Farina, driving an Alfa Romeo, won the first World Championship race here in 1950 to complete his title triumph.

The formidably steep bankings of the oval circuit characterized Monza in the fifties, yet when the protests finally brought the racing back down to ground level this remained one of the world's superfast circuits. Indeed, the average speed of Briton Peter Gethin's BRM in 1971 was 150·754 m.p.h. Chicanes however, have since been incoporated into the circuit and contained Monza's speeds within the bounds of acceptability. The fastest overall average speed of recent seasons was Nigel Mansell's 146·284 m.p.h. at the Osterreichring in 1987.

Tragedy has almost inevitably cast its shadow over Monza. Darkest day of all was in 1961, when Wolfgang von Trips's Ferrari went off the circuit, killing the German and thirteen spectators. Jim Clark was involved in the incident and amid the scenes of anguish and the clamour for retribution, there were calls for him to be thrown in jail. He had to be smuggled from the circuit and was flown out of the country by Jack Brabham. In 1970, Jochen Rindt was killed during practice (he was confirmed Champion posthumously), and in 1978 Ronnie Peterson died the day after a ten-car pile-up.

Thankfully, not all Monza's memories are sad ones. The circuit has put on some stupendous races, crowned some great champions and had some historic landmarks. In 1960, Phil Hill became the first American to win the title with a Ferrari victory that was also the last for a front-engined car. Jim Clark returned to win the race and his first Championship in 1963, and in 1972 Brazilian Emerson Fittipaldi's

success made him, at the age of twenty-five, the youngest-ever World Champion.

When Jackie Stewart drove his Matra to victory in 1969 – the first of his three Championship seasons – the first four cars were covered by a mere 0·19 seconds. Gethin had to be quick to win that race in 1971. He crossed the line just 0·01 seconds ahead of Peterson's March, and this time 0·18 seconds covered the first four, with the fifth only a further half a second adrift.

The Gethin–Peterson finish is officially recorded as the closest in history, though as times were then taken to only hundredths of a second it cannot be known whether it was in fact closer than the Ayrton Senna–Nigel Mansell margin in Spain, 1986, which was clocked at 0·014 seconds.

For the locals, of course, nothing is more thrilling than a Ferrari victory, and they won't mind stretching a point to claim it. Take 1982. René Arnoux, driving a Renault, won from Ferrari pair Patrick Tambay and Mario Andretti. But Arnoux had been signed up by Maranello for the following year, so the sports paper, *La Gazzetta dello Sport*, had no compunction proclaiming: 'Ferrari 1–2–3'. Nigel Mansell has had second and third places with Williams here. There could be no better time than now, driving a Ferrari, to take that first place and complete the set.

Emerson Fittipaldi wins in 1972 – becoming the youngest ever World Champion

MONZA is, in every sense, a remarkable place. Its history and its atmosphere make it very, very special. The crowds are incredible both in terms of numbers and enthusiasm. They are truly fanatical. They are different from any other fans in the world, and I'm glad to say that now they are on my side. Far better to have them with you than against you.

The scenes at the end of the race, when they invade the track, are accepted as part of the Italian Grand Prix. You also have to accept that unless you are careful you're going to have things taken away by souvenir hunters. It's renowned for things going missing. Whole sets of wheels have gone overnight. They'll take bits of bodywork, wings, anything.

It's about the only place in the world that has spiked guardrails round the pit and paddock area. Even then the fans somehow get in. If you leave your car out on the circuit you're really asking for trouble. Within half an hour it can have been stripped and carried off in bits in various directions. It's quite funny – as long as it's not your car.

But for all that it's a tremendously exciting place and, as a driver, you have to respond to it. Although the facilities have, for some years, needed updating, the actual setting is very attractive. The park is beautiful, and usually the weather is fine. The food is always good, and so is the local golf course.

This is one of the extremely fast tracks, even with the chicanes. It's very distinctive, too. Nicely laid out. There are some corners – the Lesmo pair, the Parabolica and the back chicane – where you definitely hold on tight. Concentration is vital there. It's hard on the cars because the kerbs are just low enough to go on, and you have to go on them for a quick time. But that can cause damage.

For the driver it's not particularly tough overall in terms of work-rate, yet it is still a driving challenge and it's very satisfying when you've produced a good lap. I've done reasonably well here, but it's one of the circuits where I haven't so far won. Hopefully I can put that right. I don't think the fans will mind if I do!

Lap of Monza

Crossing the start/finish line you are travelling very quickly indeed. You are up into sixth, and the track is so wide that overtaking is no problem at all providing you have the power! If the overtaking car happens to be a Ferrari the crowd in the grandstands opposite the pits are up on their feet, screaming and waving. It's a fantastic sight.

The cars are doing up to 210 m.p.h. before the first set of chicanes. From this great open straight it's suddenly very tight. You are braking hard and changing down to second gear. This is where we have the first encounter with those low kerbs, and this is the feature of Monza

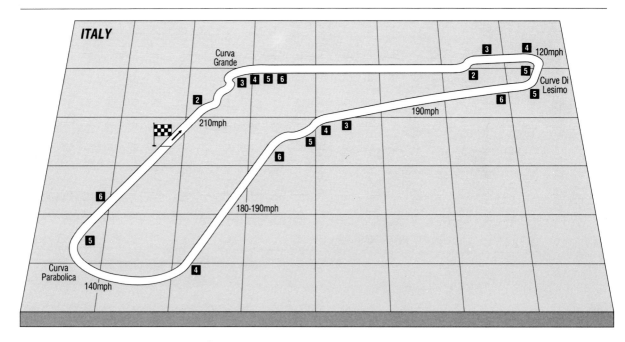

I am not keen on. As I've said, you have to bounce over the kerbs if you are to put in a competitive time, but I don't think that is purist driving. It is a necessity, and you have to put up with it here.

Down to second then, and squeezing through the chicane. Needless to say it can be particularly tricky here from the start. Everyone has rushed down from the grid only to come to this chicane. You have to sort yourselves out without losing a wing or something. There's plenty of track ahead in which to win the race.

You are up to third as you are going through the chicane and heading for the long right-hander, the Curva Grande. Up from third, to fourth, to fifth, to sixth as you sweep right and come out onto a shortish straight. Ahead now is another chicane, a left-right.

For me this is the hardest corner on the circuit. It's very slow, taken in second or third gear. It is always dusty on this part of the circuit, and I never seem to be able to get enough grip. I'm always on tenterhooks going through here, wondering whether the car is going to get away. No matter how many times I try, no matter what line I take, I'm never satisfied that I have got it right.

Assuming you manage to get through here, you are changing up, third, fourth, and heading into a set of corners that are fantastic, among the best anywhere in the world. The two Lesmo corners are right-handers. You take the first in fourth, flat out, hanging on very tightly, probably doing 120-plus m.p.h. Then, between the two corners, you snatch fifth gear. You take the second Lesmo corner absolutely flat in fifth.

It's a very exciting corner, but very demanding. You really have to swallow hard the first few times you go through. It is so daunting because it comes back on itself. If you don't get it right, you can easily spin and hit the barriers. I've come close to having moments here, but fortunately got away with it. I can recall John Watson having a big accident here in 1981. He spun, went into the barriers, and the

Above: *On the outside looking in*

Right: *. . . and one method used to keep them there*

engine broke off the back of the car. But John was unhurt. He was very lucky.

You're out of the second Lesmo corner flat in fifth and snatching sixth as you set out along the back straight. Down here you go beneath the old circuit, flat out, reaching speeds of 190 m.p.h. or so, into one of the fastest chicanes in Grand Prix racing. It is also very distinctive.

You change down to third gear just for the entry. Then you are up into fourth and, at the exit, you've got fifth. You have actually changed gear twice within the chicane itself. That's why it is very fast and very rare. Again, it is a terrific challenge, and you feel good when you know you have got it right.

On the exit, flat in fifth, and a little way down the straight you're into sixth. This is the fourth and final straight on the circuit, and here you're doing 180 to 190 m.p.h. Not for too long, though, because you are now heading for another incredible corner, the Parabolica.

It's a right-hander, basically a 180-degree turn, but very fast. You go into it flat out in sixth gear, brake just a little bit, change down to fifth or fourth, depending on your gear ratios, and then literally hang on for all you're worth. It's a huge corner that comes back on itself. It is similar to the last corner in Mexico, though not that fast. But you're still doing about 140 m.p.h., and speeding up all the way through the corner. It's a sling-shot out onto the main straight again. You're up, fifth to sixth, for this is the fastest part of the circuit, even if there are a few bumps, and back across the start/finish line.

Monza Fact file

Circuit length: 3·604 miles, 5·800 km.
Race distance: 51 laps (183·804 miles, 295·880 km.)
Qualifying lap record: Nelson Piquet (Williams Honda) 1m. 23·460s., in 1987
Race lap record: Ayrton Senna (Lotus Honda) 1m. 26·796s. at 149·479 m.p.h., in 1987

Winners: 1950, Guiseppe Farina (Alfa Romeo); 1951, Alberto Ascari (Ferrari); 1952, Alberto Ascari (Ferrari); 1953, Juan-Manuel Fangio (Maserati); 1954, Juan-Manuel Fangio (Mercedes-Benz); 1955, Juan-Manuel Fangio (Mercedes-Benz); 1956, Stirling Moss (Maserati); 1957, Stirling Moss (Vanwall); 1958, Tony Brooks (Vanwall); 1959, Stirling Moss (Cooper-Climax); 1960, Phil Hill (Ferrari); 1961, Phil Hill (Ferrari); 1962, Graham Hill (BRM); 1963, Jim Clark (Lotus Climax); 1964, John Surtees (Ferrari); 1965, Jackie Stewart (BRM); 1966, Ludovico Scarfiotti (Ferrari); 1967, John Surtees (Honda); 1968, Denny Hulme (McLaren Ford); 1969, Jackie Stewart (Matra Ford); 1970, Clay Regazzoni (Ferrari); 1971, Peter Gethin (BRM); 1972, Emerson Fittipaldi (Lotus Ford); 1973, Ronnie Peterson (Lotus Ford); 1974, Ronnie Peterson (Lotus Ford); 1975, Clay Regazzoni (Ferrari); 1976, Ronnie Peterson (March); 1977, Mario Andretti (Lotus Ford); 1978, Niki Lauda (Brabham-Alfa Romeo); 1979, Jody Scheckter (Ferrari); 1981, Alain Prost (Renault);, 1982, René Arnoux (Renault); 1983, Nelson Piquet (Brabham BMW); 1984, Niki Lauda (McLaren TAG); 1985, Alain Prost (McLaren TAG); 1986, Nelson Piquet (Williams Honda); 1987, Nelson Piquet (Williams Honda); 1988, Gerhard Berger (Ferrari)

Nigel Mansell: 1981, retired (Lotus Ford); 1982, 7th (Lotus Ford); 1983, 8th (Lotus Renault); 1984, accident (Lotus Renault); 1985, retired (Williams Honda); 1986, 2nd (Williams Honda); 1987, 3rd (Williams Honda); 1988, did not enter (Williams Judd)

13 PORTUGAL

Circuit: Estoril

From Monza the Formula One roadshow travels across Europe and across the spectrum of racing settings. For those who find the din, the hype and the pandemonium of the old hotbed a little too much, the Iberian sector of the season provides suitable relief. Two of the newer venues, they are, by comparison with Italy, low-key, quite docile affairs.

Ahead is the Spanish Grand Prix at Jerez, but first it's the Portuguese race, held up in the rolling scrubland four miles inland from Estoril and twenty miles from the splendid yet still largely undiscovered capital, Lisbon. Westward along the Atlantic coast, just beyond Estoril, is the busy little resort of Cascais. Beyond the shops, bars and restaurants, its origins as a fishing village are still apparent.

Venture further still, past the pottery, and the linen and woollen stalls; here the coast is rugged and unspoiled, life good and uncomplicated. Breathe in that sea air and clear your system of all that Monza mania. Around this corner, too, you may find one or two of the Formula One drivers, playing golf or simply lazing.

The holiday mood may not persist all the way to the racing track, but it does tend to set the tempo for the weekend. Since Portuguese Formula One drivers are not too thick on the ground, the local support is usually for the Brazilians. The Brits may be old allies and are well received but Brazilians are family, after all.

It was a celebrated Brit who won the first two Portuguese Grands Prix, though neither was held in these parts. In 1958, Stirling Moss had to defy the tramlines and cobblestones as well as the opposition in Oporto to steer his Vanwall to victory. The following year, different car (Cooper-Climax), different circuit (Lisbon's Monsanto Park), but the same master. When the race went back to Oporto in 1960, however, Jack Brabham was at the wheel of the triumphant Cooper-Climax.

For twenty-four subsequent years, Portugal was in the Grand Prix wilderness. A new circuit did appear in the seventies. It staged European Formula Two Championship races. But without adequate and regular maintenance work it rapidly deteriorated. It was occasionally used as a special stage for the Portuguese rally, but for little else.

Then, in the early eighties, the Portuguese drew up ambitious plans to refurbish and modernize the circuit. On 21 October 1984, their dreams became reality when the updated Autodromo do Estoril staged the return of the Portuguese Grand Prix, and since then the race has become a regular fixture.

The new generation of drivers found a circuit generally to their liking. It was bumpy in parts, dirty and therefore quite slippery, too. But its varied contours and corners make it both interesting and testing. The driver has to work for his corn and his points. A main straight more than

Right: *Gerhard Berger negotiates Turn 5 in 1987*

half a mile long and a quick back stretch balance the tight, twisty sections to put this circuit into the medium-speed range.

The history of Estoril's Grand Prix circuit may be relatively short, but it is eventful and, in the wider context of the sport, most significant. That first race here was the final round of the 1984 Championship and the deciding encounter for the driver's title. The constructors' contest had been dominated by the record-breaking McLaren team and now their drivers, Niki Lauda and Alain Prost, were locked in a fascinating duel for the individual crown.

Lauda, the old fox, couldn't compete with the out-and-out-pace of Prost that season, but he had the cunning and patience to pick up what was required from the races. So they went into the Portuguese Grand Prix knowing that even if Prost won, second place would be good enough to give the Austrian his third Championship.

Prost started from second place on the grid, while Lauda was way down in eleventh spot. The Frenchman took the lead on lap nine, and from that point his seventh victory of the season was scarcely in doubt. What mattered now was Lauda's progress. He carved his way through the field to third place but still that wasn't sufficient, and in front of him was a determined Nigel Mansell, driving his last race for Lotus.

Left: *Champion again . . . Lauda and the team-mate who has to wait*

Right: *Senna masters the wet for his first win, in 1985*

Then, suddenly, the brakes of the Lotus went and Lauda was through. The title was his by a mere half a point. On the podium he consoled his team-mate. Lauda recalls: 'He was fighting back the tears. I told him to forget it. Forget it as soon as he could. That was my year. The next would be his.' And so it was.

The Portuguese race that following year belonged to Ayrton Senna. Undeterred by the atrocious, wet conditions, he registered his first Grand Prix win in the Lotus. Nigel Mansell, now with Williams, started from the pit lane yet finished a fine fifth.

Nigel's most glorious day here, however, was to come in 1986. He produced one of the outstanding, authoritative performances of his career to win from Prost and Piquet, and give himself a ten-point lead in the World Championship standings with just two Grands Prix remaining.

In 1987 Prost took advantage of Gerhard Berger's slip to establish an all-time record of twenty-eight Grand Prix wins. The little man was at the top of the podium again in 1988 after being almost pressed up against the pit wall by McLaren partner Senna. 'I had to speak to him after that,' said Prost. There was also a rousing Mansell-Senna scrap that afternoon, which ended, alas, when the Englishman went off avoiding a backmarker.

CERTAINLY a lot seems to have happened in the few years we've been coming to Estoril. That 1984 Grand Prix was an amazing first race for any circuit to have, and every season since there has been plenty to talk about here. Fortunately, I've been able to win here, and that was one of my most satisfying races. I opened a gap and then held it. I didn't push too hard, but controlled it from the front.

I've generally gone fairly well here. The brakes, as I feared, let me down when I was running second in 1984 and allowed Niki to pip Alain for the Championship. It was a horrendous day here in 1985, and I was one of the three drivers who started from the pit lane. I managed to battle my way through to pick up a couple of points. I was again running second, feeling very comfortable, behind Gerhard in 1987 when my car just died on me. In 1988 I was having a real ding-dong with Ayrton. We both had to go off to miss a backmarker. Ayrton was lucky and got back on. I wasn't and didn't. But again, it was good stuff.

It is an interesting circuit, a driver's circuit, so that always gives you a chance of getting a good race. In fact the whole area is pleasant and very relaxing. I usually stay along the coast from Cascais at Quinta. There's a golf course right there and, if work permits, I try to get in a couple of rounds over the weekend. It's good just to be by the sea. It is very soothing, and that is something that can prove useful if you've had a hard day at the track. It can help recharge the batteries. I have plenty of golfing interests in Portugal because I am now President of the Pine Cliff Golf and Country Club on the Algarve.

The circuit can be demanding, too. It's tough on the car, tough on the gearbox and reasonably tough on the man. There are some parts where you have to work particularly hard and have to hang on. There are some very fast corners, very difficult corners. The one into the pit straight is probably one of the highest G-loading corners we have.

It is a circuit with a lot of character. It climbs and it descends. It's quite bumpy in places, and the car has to be set up just right to be competitive. It's quite a dirty track, a lot of dust about the place. That can be even more of a problem when the wind blows – and here it can and does! The surface conditions at the corners can change from lap to lap. On the same line you can have good grip one lap, and then virtually no grip at all on the next. That can put you in big trouble.

Much of the circuit is quite tight, though the main straight is long and here you can reach 190 m.p.h. Along here there is obviously an opportunity for overtaking, and it's important to grab it. There are a couple of other places where you might get by, but you are depending on the other driver making a mistake. If you can qualify well and earn a good grid position it makes life easier.

This is, though, a nice circuit and one I enjoy coming to. You can really enjoy the *driving* here, which makes a good lap or race all the more satisfying. Any driver likes to come away from a racing track knowing he's done a good job and got as much out of the car as is possible. When you've gone well here you have that sort of feeling.

Above: Out on his own . . . Mansell on course for victory, 1986

Right: *Mansell leads from the grid, 1987*

Lap of Estoril

Coming out of that final corner you are up to sixth gear and flat out as you cross the start/finish line. This main straight provides the chance to take advantage of your power if you have it and, of course, the best opportunity for overtaking manoeuvres. You can be reaching 190 m.p.h. towards the end of the straight.

For Turn 1, by the Pirelli Bridge, you change down to fifth and go through the corner flat out, staying in fifth, at about 140 m.p.h. Still keeping it in fifth, you go into Turn 2, another right-hander. Depending on how brave you are – or how foolish you are – you may try to go through here flat out, without lifting. Sometimes a confidence lift is required. That will be dictated by how much grip you feel the car has in the corner. Even so, Turn 2 is considerably quicker than Turn 1; probably 150 to 160 m.p.h.

Out of Turn 2, you stay in fifth or you might change up to sixth, depending on your gear ratios. In the past I have set my gears to keep in fifth all the way down to Turn 3, which is a tight, double-apex right-hander. Changing and braking very hard, down to third, you want to be very tight on the first apex and then slide out of it so that you can just hit the second apex and turn in.

Keep in third to Turn 4, braking hard and changing down to second. A reasonably tight hairpin, speed of about 70 m.p.h. Coming out of here you are flat out, second, third, fourth, fifth. Still in fifth for Turn

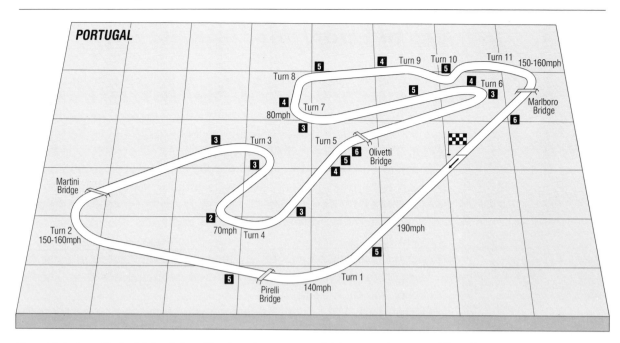

5, which is a little kink right. You're flat out, and it's very bumpy. If you are too close to the inside, you will be pushed across the circuit.

Coming out of the kink you snatch sixth, and then it's flat out, hard on towards Turn 6. You try to brake as late as you can, change down to third and almost throw the car into the corner. It's a double-apex left. It's very tight on the first turn, and then the second apex opens right out. You change gear halfway through the corner to fourth. Then it's fifth, and flat down a short straight to Turn 7.

A right-hand corner, braking fairly hard, down to third and through at about 80 m.p.h. Sliding out, up to fourth and up a short straight. You can stay in fourth for the next corner as long as you get it right. Turn 8 is quite a sharp right-hander. You have got to be very precise on hitting the apex here, because if you hit the kerb or get too close it throws you across the circuit. You can finish up in the barrier on the outside. It's a tight corner, but if you get it right you can make up valuable time.

Again, at Turn 9, you can go round in fourth and, if your tyres are gripping the way you would want them to, you can hold fourth for both 9 and 10. They are very close together, a right, then a left. That's what I did in qualifying in 1988. You have to take care. There is only one line. You don't want to hit the kerbs and make the car unstable. You need the car as stable as possible to go through 9 and 10 at about 90 to 100, and 110 to 120 m.p.h.

Turn 10 then throws you into this incredible last corner. Before you enter you're flat in fifth, and you take the right-hander in fifth, which brings you up to a speed of 150 to 160 m.p.h. You have to keep it very close to the inside, letting it drift out, then bringing it back to the inside. You are fighting the car all the way round. The G-load increases all the way round too, until you go under the Marlboro Bridge and take sixth gear to head back down the main straight, across the start/finish line.

Right: *Rolling scrubland, drivers' circuit*

Estoril Fact file

Circuit length: 2·703 miles, 4·350 km.
Race distance: 70 laps (189·207 miles, 304·500 km.)
Qualifying lap record: Ayrton Senna (Lotus Renault) 1m. 16·673s., in 1986
Race lap record: Gerhard Berger (Ferrari) 1m. 19·282s., at 122·734 m.p.h., in 1987

Winners: 1984, Alain Prost (McLaren TAG); 1985, Ayrton Senna (Lotus Renault); 1986, Nigel Mansell (Williams Honda); 1987, Alain Prost (McLaren TAG); 1988, Alain Prost (McLaren Honda)

Nigel Mansell: 1984, retired (Lotus Renault); 1985, 5th (Williams Honda); 1986, 1st (Williams Honda); 1987, retired (Williams Honda); 1988, accident (Williams Judd)

14 SPAIN

Circuit: Jerez de la Frontera

The great European tour has now made its final destination the southwest corner of Spain. The crowds that had dwindled by Estoril have all but disappeared by the time we reach the plains of Andalucia. The mayor of Jerez thought a Grand Prix racetrack would give the city and its sherry a new shop window. Formula One and television arrived in 1986, but so far José Public has shown a distinct reluctance to turn over his hard-earned pesetas at the turnstiles.

The lack of a major conurbation, and convenient flights and accommodation do not help the cause. More's the pity, because this site just to the east of Jerez was chosen with the spectator very much in mind. The circuit snakes between hills and banks that give some of the best views of Grand Prix action anywhere in the world. And action there has been. The first three races here have provided incident and high drama.

It's not that Spain doesn't have a tradition in the sport. The first recorded 'Grand Prix' was way back in 1913. It was held at Guadarrama and won by Carlos de Salamanca, driving a Rolls-Royce! San Sebastian was the main centre between the wars, but the first World Championship Spanish Grand Prix, in 1951, was contested on the Pedralbes street circuit in Barcelona. Victory in that final race of the season went to the new champion, Juan-Manuel Fangio, in an Alfa Romeo.

Spain had to wait until 1954 for its next Grand Prix, and again Pedralbes was the scene. This time the Ferrari of Mike Hawthorn led the way, beginning a sequence of five victories for British drivers on Spanish soil. You can make that six if you throw in Jim Clark's non-Championship success. The other triumphant Brits were Graham Hill (once) and Jackie Stewart (three times).

From the late sixties to 1975 the race alternated between Jarama, near Madrid, and the attractive Montjuich Park circuit in Barcelona. The race never returned to Montjuich after five spectators were killed by German Rolf Stommelen's Lola. Jarama became the regular stage until its final act in 1981. It was also Gilles Villeneuve's final win. For lap after tantalizing lap he kept his Ferrari ahead of the pack snarling at his heels.

Jerez's enterprise put Spain back on the Grand Prix map in April, 1986. The new hosts opened their arms and their bodegas to Formula One. There was sherry tasting and flamenco dancing; they served up demonstrations of horsemanship and course after extravagant course at banquets that meandered on into the small hours. At the circuit there were wall-to-wall Tio Pepe girls, smartly attired in red and black.

There were probably more Tio Pepe girls than spectators when the cars rolled out into warm spring sunshine for practice. (The race has since been sensibly slotted into the calendar a week after Portugal.) They picked their way around a circuit they found to be basically slow. There

Right: *The circuit snakes between hills and banks*

were lots of slow corners; tight and twisty sections. But there were some quick, challenging parts, too, particularly behind the paddock, before the hairpin that released them onto the main straight.

Working facilities for the teams were good. There was plenty of space in the garages and the paddock. Access was no problem, either. There still seems little danger of traffic jams into the night down in these parts. You had to pinch yourself to believe there really was going to be a Grand Prix there that weekend.

The stage, if not the audience, was set, and it was a premiere worthy of any theatre. A charging Nigel Mansell came up behind Ayrton Senna on the last corner, and as both lunged for the line the clock gave the verdict to the Brazilian's Lotus by 0·014 seconds. The distance was calculated at a mere ninety-three centimetres.

There was spectacular jousting in 1987 as well, but on this occasion all the competition was for the places. From first to last the race was controlled by Mansell in the Williams. Much as he had done in Portugal the year before, he gave himself a cushion and rested on it with utter self-assurance. It was his twelfth Grand Prix win in a period of two years, and it kept alive his Championship hopes for that season.

In 1988 Nigel, driving the normally aspirated Williams Judd, was chasing victory again, but Prost and his McLaren Honda resisted all. Still, it was another good Jerez result for the Englishman. Three races had yielded a first and two seconds. He has good cause to like the place. In his last season at Williams, a variety of mishaps restricted him to two finishes. Each time he came in second behind a McLaren.

Great view, few viewers

J UST like Portugal, it's a new circuit that has already had quite a big impact. There have been good, exciting races here and obviously from a personal point of view they've been very enjoyable. Good decision to come down here, I say. Smashing place. I think it would be very sad if they changed this race for one somewhere else!

Seriously, though, it is a nice circuit and a challenging circuit. It is perhaps not as nice as Estoril, but it has been well planned for both the driver and the spectator. You have to work and concentrate all the time here. It is a long race, a hard race. You know you've done a job of work when you've finished.

With so many slow corners you've got to get the balance of the car right. You need the downforce here. It can also be pretty hard on tyres. Grip is a problem anyway because it's another dusty circuit. You seem to be constantly searching for grip. You can also have a difficult search for somewhere to overtake, as I know only too well. It's more twisty than Estoril, so you really don't want to be too far down the starting grid.

It's a great shame they don't get bigger crowds here, because it's an excellent circuit from a spectator's point of view. It's possible to see two or three parts of the circuit from one position. But the lack of a big crowd atmosphere doesn't really affect the drivers. They are too busy fighting the circuit to be concerned with the crowd. My attitude is that you have to be blinkered and just get on with the job. Having said that, I'm sure I'll notice the Ferrari crowd!

First corner . . . a tight right-hander

An advantage of a circuit this far south in Europe is that it gives the Formula One teams another option for winter testing. The English and North European tracks can be very bleak and it's obviously not possible to keep going to places like Brazil and South Africa. Ricard has often been used, and now Estoril and Jerez are popular choices.

Testing is part of the job no one sees. The days are long and the work can be tedious. But this is where you can find that fraction of a second that makes all the difference come race weekend.

It was at Jerez that I had my first drive following my big accident in Japan. I hadn't been on track for 108 days when I came here to test the Williams Judd in February, 1988. I was still recovering from a back injury, and I had aches and pains all that week. But the job had to be done and for me it was important to be in a car again.

Jerez, then, is another good, challenging circuit, where the driver has the opportunity to show his ability. Get it all together here and you are entitled to feel satisfied with your efforts.

Lap of Jerez

Coming onto the main straight, past the start/finish line, you're up to sixth gear. Towards the end of the straight you're up to 180 or 190 m.p.h. The track also rises a little just here as you come into the first corner, a tight right-hander. You're down to third gear, braking hard, and going through the corner at 80 to 90 m.p.h. Now you're going down a short straight, you're up into fourth gear, before braking hard for the Michelin Corner.

This is a second-gear corner. Very hard round this one. You want to keep it as tight as you can here. Up from second to third to fourth gear, coming out very quickly because ahead now is a sequence of four bends that you can take flat out in fifth. It's an incredible, flowing section.

You must have a really good balance on the car for this. The bends are quite tight and you take the last one at, I would say, 150 m.p.h. You certainly wouldn't wish to get it wrong, because there's not much of a run-off area. Could be rather nasty. Just touching the brakes for the right-hander down to fourth, and then flat out round the corner.

That brings you into a chicane. You can take this in third or fourth, depending on your gear ratios. You're going through the chicane at about 90 to 100 m.p.h. Exiting down a little straight on which you can

'A long race, a hard race'

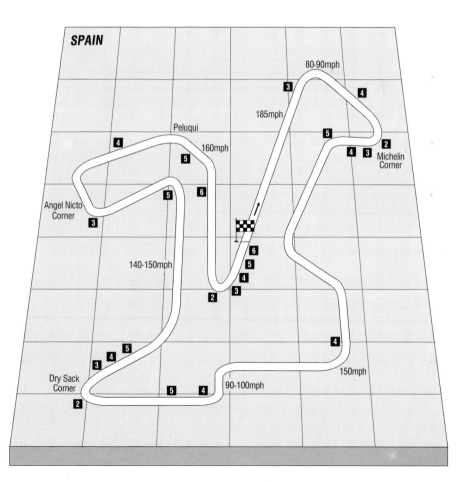

Mansell takes the chequered flag, 1987

get back up to fifth before the Dry Sack Corner. This is a right-hander, second or third gear, again depending on ratios.

As soon as you exit this corner you have to be quickly up through the gears: second, third, fourth, fifth. You are suddenly into a left-hander. Again, it's flat out and very demanding. You can sometimes hit the rev limiter in fifth if you go through it very quickly. You are soon entering a long, long left-hander, which is also taken in fifth. These two corners are taken at about 140 to 150 m.p.h. You have to hang on. Very tricky. You mustn't go too wide on the second corner.

Out of the left-hander it's down a short straight, still flat out in fifth gear, to the Angel Nicto Corner. For this right-hand corner you change down to fourth or third (depending on ratios). Here again, you have to keep it very tight, then you slide to the outside. Fourth gear before the next corner. This is Peluqui, a right-hander. No braking here, just accelerating through the corner as fast as you can.

Changing up now as you come down what is really the back straight with two right kinks in it. You go from fourth to fifth to sixth, and down the back straight flat out. This section takes you round the back of the pits and paddock area. It's a very spectacular section and an excellent part to be watching.

I would say, the first corner, or kink, is the harder to take flat out because there's a big bump in the middle of it, which throws you to the outside of the circuit. If the car isn't totally stable you really do think you are being thrown off. As long as the car has got through

Jerez's spacious paddock

the first right-hander all right, you know you can take the second flat out. Not comfortably, but then these corners are taken at 160-plus m.p.h.

Coming out of the second right-hander, it's a sling-shot down another short straight, which takes you to the hairpin before the main straight. Here you are braking very hard and changing down to second gear. Just on the exit you take third, and you're going through the gears as you rush for the start/finish line.

It was at the hairpin that I was right behind Senna in 1986, and though I came inside him along the straight I didn't quite have enough road. The funny thing is that the start/finish line had been moved back from its original position. That extra stretch would have been just about enough. Still, it was a tremendous finish, and I can't complain about my results here. Hopefully I can look forward to more of the same.

Jerez Fact file

Circuit length: 2·621 miles, 4·218 km.
Race distance: 72 laps (188·708 miles, 303·696 km.)
Qualifying lap record: Ayrton Senna (Lotus Renault) 1m. 21·605s., in 1986
Race lap record: Gerhard Berger (Ferrari) 1m. 26·986s., at 108·489 m.p.h., in 1987

Winners: 1986, Ayrton Senna (Lotus Renault); 1987, Nigel Mansell (Williams Honda); 1988, Alain Prost (McLaren Honda)

Nigel Mansell: 1986, 2nd (Williams Honda); 1987, 1st (Williams Honda); 1988, 2nd (Williams Judd)

15 JAPAN

Circuit: *Suzuka*

Considering the enormous Japanese influence in modern Formula One, the wonder is it took them so long to reclaim a date on the World Championship calendar. The nation that staged races in 1976 and 1977 bowed its greetings again in 1987. During the interim decade Japan had injected vital sponsorship money into the sport. The likes of Canon and Leyton House recognized and responded to the massive potential. The Norfolk based Lotus team even hired a Japanese driver, in the shape of Satoru Nakajima.

But then that signing was part of a package that enabled Lotus to share the benefits of the most significant Japanese impact on Grand Prix motor racing. That, of course, was the Honda engine. Honda's return, in partnership with Williams, was devastating. Their cars, driven by Nigel

Below: *Lauda gives up in the wet, Fuji, 1976*

Mansell and Nelson Piquet, romped away with the Constructors' Championship in 1986 and 1987.

It was to Hondaland, a Japanese leisure complex featuring the Suzuka circuit and owned by the company, that the Formula One band ventured in the autumn of 1987. That weekend – like the Japanese Grand Prix weekend of 1988 – proved decisive to the drivers' title. Such, though, was the tradition of the race.

Japan's first Championship race was the last of the 1976 season, and when the show arrived at Mount Fuji the principals were Niki Lauda, back after his appalling accident at the Nürburgring, and Britain's James Hunt. Lauda quit in the deluge, and Hunt managed the third place that gave him the crown by one point.

Below right: . . . and Hunt carries on to become Champion

Let Lauda take you back to that memorable day: 'The feeling is absolutely unbearable, sitting there panic-stricken, rain lashing down, seeing nothing, just hunched down in the cockpit, shoulders tense, waiting for someone to run into you. Everybody is skating and spinning; it is crazy. Looking at it this way, it seems only sensible to drive into the pits and give up.'

The following year Hunt won the race but Lauda, in perfect reply to his critics, had already secured his second Championship. Sporting events that day were, in any case, overshadowed by the consequences of an accident involving Gilles Villeneuve and Ronnie Peterson. Villeneuve's Ferrari left the track, killing two spectators. It was the end of the Japanese Grand Prix at Fuji.

The Suzuka circuit is thirty miles from Nagoya and ninety miles east of Osaka. It was built in 1961, and has regularly staged Formula Two and Formula 3000 races. It has also been the test ground for Honda in their meticulously planned campaign to shift the balance of power in Formula One.

This may not be one of the world's great beauty spots, though since you're likely to spend all your time getting from hotel to circuit, back to hotel and finding a meal before Japan closes, it scarcely matters. Unless you know the way or have a degree in Japanese, driving is not recommended. Trying to read the road signs can be more infuriating and ultimately less productive than sitting in a queue.

Prices, too, can be daunting, especially if you insist on your fillet steak and ample European hotel room. If you settle for Japanese accommodation be prepared for something on the small side. The drivers at least have the convenience and comfort offered by the hotel at the circuit.

The circuit has the uncommon feature of a cross-over, giving it a basic figure eight layout. The start/finish line is on the clockwise section, which runs as far as the underpass and the beginning of the anti-clockwise part. The cars swing back towards the bridge at the Spoon Curve, which has been modified, and turn into the start/finish straight after the chicane, which was added in 1983.

Suzuka has some fast stretches and corners, but the chicane and some slower corners bring down the average speeds to the fast-medium range. They also mean there is little respite for the driver. Overtaking is not easy, concentration vital. But like all challenges, it offers the incentive of job satisfaction.

General reaction to the circuit and its facilities has been favourable Gerhard Berger was even moved to say: 'I liked it straight away. I like it as much as any other circuit in the world. Nigel Mansell showed me the line because he knew it from testing, and after that it was good. I got pole position and then won the race.'

It was not so good for Nigel that first year. He had a bad accident during the first qualifying session, his car crashing backwards into the barrier, then being thrown into the air and across the track again. He suffered serious back injuries which put him out of that race, out of the final race in Australia and, of course, out of the World Championship contest.

'There are some difficult corners'

The title went to his team-mate Nelson Piquet who, ironically, didn't manage another point from the last two Grands Prix. For the second successive season, Nigel had to settle for the runner-up spot, even though he had won more races than any other driver.

In 1988 Honda, now with McLaren, had the one-two and the title clincher they wanted. Ayrton Senna, despite fluffing his start, roared back to beat Alain Prost in the drizzle and take the crown. Nigel, too, put on a charge after losing his nose-cone in a collision with Derek Warwick, only to be forced out after a coming-together with Piquet. The Williams flipped at an alarming angle into the air, but came down on its wheels.

T HIS has certainly not been the happiest of tracks for me so far. The accident in 1987 put me out of the Championship and left me with the most painful injuries I have had. I had spinal concussion and a couple of fractured ribs. I was told by the specialist to rest, and that's exactly what I did for two months.

You naturally think about whether it's worth going on in a situation like that. I did, after all, have a lot of time to think. But I decided that it was no time to give in. I had achieved quite a bit, and I felt I could do more. Through the winter I built up my training and had a tough stint at a health clinic in Austria. I was back in a car at that test session in Spain.

In 1988, I made the race all right, but that early altercation with Derek Warwick cost me a nose-cone for the first time in my Formula One career. I got that replaced and went on a charge, only to come upon Nelson when he was obviously not quite with it. He'd been ill that weekend and he was clearly struggling in the race. He was a lap down on me and when I came up behind him he didn't know where he was, let alone where I was.

Suddenly we have collided and I'm tipped up into the air at a very nasty angle. Luckily I come down the right way and am just a little shaken. The car, though, is finished. The suspension is damaged and I can't go on. Not surprisingly, Nelson didn't go on much longer, either. He was too sick to continue.

So no, not the happiest of memories from Suzuka. What with the incidents on the track and developments off it, which cost us Honda engines for 1988, my Japanese connection seems fated. You can't

Suzuka enters the Formula 1 World Championship

afford to let these things get you down, though. Racing has its setbacks like anything else. It's the next race that matters and the next race you look forward to.

I think it's fair to say that in 1987 I made the mistake of not going out to Japan early enough. I knew the circuit reasonably well from testing there with Honda. But we're talking about travelling to the other side of the world. Almost to a different world. You must give yourself enough time to acclimatize, to settle in, otherwise you can injure yourself trying to do the job properly. So in 1988 I gave myself more time and then went on to Australia. It makes much more sense to combine the two.

The biggest problem here is the difference we come upon in terms of culture and people. It is so unlike the West in many ways. This side of the trip can be a distraction in itself. It is essential for us to stay at the Suzuka Hotel because a journey of a few miles can take you an eternity. The traffic is horrendous. And unless you know the way from memory, don't attempt it. You could be out there all day!

But you have to hand it to the Japanese people. They are so industrious, so committed to whatever they undertake, that when they say they are going to do something they do it all right and they do it well. They are very astute, very professional. Their achievements speak for themselves. They prepared very carefully for Formula One. Facilities were excellent, they laid on Western food, everything was absolutely right.

The circuit itself is good. It has gone down well with the drivers. It has plenty to extend and test the driver, and that he always appreciates. There are some difficult corners, but overall it's a fast-medium track. The cross-over is a strange feature, but by no means a problem. In fact you're not aware of other cars going over or beneath you. The barriers hide you from view. Besides, you don't have time to look around – or below. You have to keep your eyes forward and your mind on the job.

Lap of Suzuka

Coming out of the Casio Triangle and crossing the start/finish line, you're going up through the gears, second, third, fourth, fifth, sixth. The straight is unusual in that it is downhill. You are accelerating up to 200 m.p.h. before you come into the First Curve. Here, if you have the car and the power, you have an obvious overtaking opportunity.

The First Curve is a right-hander, taken in fourth gear. You accelerate all the way round. It's very quick here and it's leading you into a sequence of corners. There are five of them in all as the track snakes left and right. You take them in fourth and you take them quickly. It's one of those sections where you have to get into a rhythm. You need to get it right from the start. It's left, right, left, right, left.

It was at the first right that I went off in 1987. You daren't get

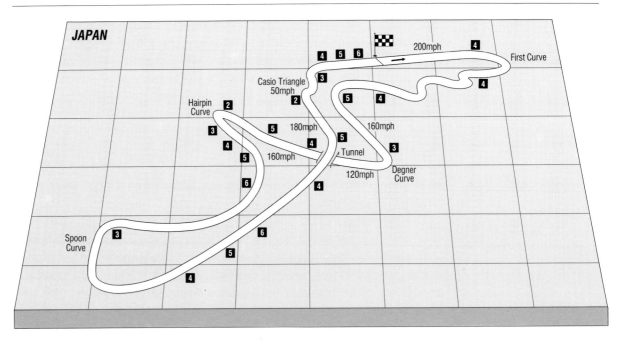

more than a couple of inches off line because you will lose grip and the back will get away. It's as simple – and costly – as that.

That's why you have to have a sort of sixth sense in racing. You are constantly on the alert, looking at the track surface for any sign of potential problems. Is there any dirt, any oil, any water? The marshals do a fantastic job, but unless something happens in front of them they can easily miss it. The first they may know about it is when a car gets into trouble and for that driver flags are out too late.

After the early S-curves in this series, you come up the hill and change to fifth for a long left-hander. This takes you to the Degner Curve, and along here you are flat out, probably getting up to 160 m.p.h. Degner Curve is a right-hander, which you take in third gear.

This brings you into the tunnel at the cross-over point, where you're doing about 120 m.p.h. and accelerating. You're going up to fourth, to fifth, again touching 160 m.p.h. Then you brake very hard for the Hairpin Curve. It's a left-hander, second gear, one of the slowest parts of the circuit. Out of here you accelerate up the hill, and along a section of the track that sweeps to the right in a long curve. You are also going up through the gears again: second, third, fourth, fifth, sixth. You're flat out in sixth heading for the Spoon Curve.

This is a very tricky corner, double apex left, with opposite camber on the second part, which means the car is constantly trying to fall away. You take this in third, accelerate through it, then change up to fourth, to fifth, to sixth, down the back main straight. Just beyond the cross-over you have a quick flick left. You get speeds of up to 180 m.p.h. here as you make for the Casio Triangle. This is the tightest corner on the course. It's also the hardest braking area. You're braking very, very hard. You are down to second gear, about 50 m.p.h. It's a right-left through the chicane, and then you're changing up through the gears again as you sweep right back onto the straight and across the line.

Right: *'Plenty to extend and test the driver'*

Suzuka Fact file

Circuit length: 3·641 miles, 5·859 km.
Race distance: 51 laps (185·670 miles, 298·809 km.)
Qualifying lap record: Gerhard Berger (Ferrari) 1m. 40·042s., in 1987
Race lap record: Alain Prost (McLaren TAG) 1m.

43·844s., at 126·210 m.p.h., in 1987

Winners: 1987, Gerhard Berger (Ferrari); 1988, Ayrton Senna (McLaren Honda)

Nigel Mansell: 1987, did not start (Williams Honda); 1988, accident (Williams Judd)

16 AUSTRALIA

Circuit: *Adelaide*

A season of drama and spectacle, joy and despair, has taken us to the other side of the world and the last of its sixteen performances. Adelaide has become a fitting stage for the Grand Prix finale; fitting in that it captures the global nature and status of the Formula One Championship; fitting in that it is an uninhibited extravaganza of celebration and fun. Jackie Stewart was even moved to describe it as 'undoubtedly now the finest Grand Prix in the world'.

Three years out of the first four here, the title had been decided before the show hit town, but it mattered not one jot. The Australian Grand Prix stands as an event in its own right. That is no doubt due in part to geography, but in part also to the Aussies' all-consuming love of living. Enthusiasm here comes by the tuckerbagful.

Adelaide is an unlikely source of such festivity. It had long had the image of the quiet, withdrawn relation among Australian cities living in the shadow of Sydney, Melbourne, Brisbane and Perth, and of its own churches. The Grand Prix has changed all that. So much so that the Formula One fraternity are regretting it took them so long to discover the place.

They can't claim that's because this is all new to Oz. There has, after all, been 'Grand Prix racing' of sorts down under for more than sixty years. The event has travelled the length and breadth of this massive country. Even to Tasmania. It all started on Phillip Island, Victoria State, in 1928. The cars came in by boat and invaded territory the penguins, not unreasonably, thought was their own. The winner was an outsider, too, an Englishman, Captain Arthur Waite, driving an Austin Seven.

The Island show became a popular attraction, but it was to be an early victim of the problems that catch up with all circuits: those of speed and safety. The race went on to tour a number of road circuits – including Lobethal, in Adelaide – and old airfields. The drivers called in at Bathurst (now famed for its Touring Car classic) and Melbourne's Albert Park. One Haig Hurst got it so horribly wrong there he careered out of the park, across a busy road and on to some flabbergasted resident's front lawn. A nice cup of tea calmed nerves all round.

The advent of purpose-built circuits took Australian single-seater racing into a new era. Warwick Farm, Sandown and Lakeside emerged. So, too, did a driver called Jack Brabham and a series called the Tasman Cup. Calder flirted with Formula One in 1980. In fact only two F1 cars turned up and one of them, a Williams driven by Australia's new world champion, Alan Jones, won with ease. Formula Pacific rules were introduced in 1981, and Roberto Moreno had the first of his three successes at Calder. The 1982 race was won by Alain Prost.

The Formula One World Championship itself arrived as a result of

Uninhibited extravaganza of celebration and fun

some determined and enterprising campaigning by Adelaide which had enlisted the support of South Australia's premier, John Bannon. They mapped out a street circuit alongside Victoria Park horse racing track, a couple of miles from the city centre. It was nothing like so tight as Monaco and Detroit and had a long main straight, Dequetteville Terrace. On Grand Prix weekend it is known as the Brabham Straight.

When the drivers first came here in 1985 they were relieved to find a good, if slightly bumpy circuit; they were impressed with the organization; and appreciative of the wholehearted welcome. The organizers thought of their old folk too, offering them trips to the country away from all those noisy cars. Any cracks in the organization have since

been filled in and little ruffles ironed out, but none of the vigour has been diluted. It has become the perfect end-of-season party.

It also provided Keke Rosberg with the perfect end to his association with Williams. The 1982 World Champion won the race after his team-mate Nigel Mansell, on a hat-trick of wins and on the front row of the grid, had to retire only one lap into the race with transmission trouble. That disappointment, however, was nothing compared with what was awaiting Nigel the following year.

This time he was going for the Championship. Third place would be sufficient, no matter what Prost or Piquet achieved. Starting on pole, he drove a sensible race, stayed out of trouble and was running third with forty-four miles to go. Then that rear tyre exploded as he steamed down Brabham Straight at 200 m.p.h. His Championship in ruins, the struggle now was for survival. Images of those few dramatic, terrifying seconds will stay in the mind forever. Prost resisted Piquet's late charge to win the race and his second successive title.

In 1987 Nigel was back home in the Isle of Man, recovering from his accident in Japan. The crown was already Piquet's and Berger repeated his Suzuka victory for Ferrari. In 1988 Prost and new champion Senna gave McLaren-Honda yet another one-two to mark the end of the turbo era. For Mansell it was farewell to Williams. He qualified a splendid third behind the McLarens, but in the race was hampered by failing brakes and eventually slid out of the action.

Keke Rosberg wins Adelaide's first Grand Prix and his last for Williams

IT would be nice actually to finish a race here! But despite my lack of luck at this circuit I have to say it's a great place to end the season. It's an incredible weekend and it doesn't make any difference if the Championship has already been decided. The Aussies put on a fantastic show and really enjoy every minute of it.

They are great sporting enthusiasts anyway. They love sport, and at the same time prepare and organize it in a very professional way. Combine those qualities, and it's not surprising you get such a good Grand Prix. The British contingent always get good support from the locals.

It is good for the sport to come to the bottom of the world because we have to be seen to be a genuine *world* Championship. Formula One broke new ground by going into Eastern Europe, and it was equally important to bring the cars and the drivers down to Australia. It's a long, long way, but I, for one, hope we keep coming back here.

Adelaide is technically a street circuit, but rather different from the traditional ones. There is far more room and it's considerably faster. I have painful memories of that long straight, of course. It still hurts me to think about it. I'm sure it always will. What made it so shattering was the feeling that it was all so unjust. I'd done everything right, the Championship was virtually mine. It wasn't like 1987 because the odds were against me then anyway. But in 1986 I had it taken out of my hands.

It's easy to lump street circuits together and give the impression they are all the same, but take a closer look at Monaco, Detroit and Adelaide and you'll realize how much they can vary. The Monaco track is surrounded by barriers or houses or concrete walls. Along the waterfront at Detroit it was open but for a low concrete wall, so you had the problem of wind and dust and paper swirling about. There's no such problem at Monaco.

Adelaide is different again because it has far more of the characteristics of a purpose-built racing track. There are still some tight corners, in keeping with the usual street circuit, but there are wider corners, too, and that long straight gives you ample overtaking opportunity. It's really somewhere between the two: a good, testing blend.

It is a long race here and, despite that main straight, you are working hard most of the time. If it's hot – as it can be – you're likely to be whacked at the end of the race. Or at least that is what I've been told! It can be tough on the equipment, as well. I can certainly vouch for the fact that you can have problems with tyres and brakes.

I had hoped to finish with Williams on a high note but it wasn't to be. It wasn't, however, the end of my sporting year and I had a more gratifying competition a couple of weekends later. That was at the Royal Sydney Golf Club, where I'd entered for the Australian Open Championship.

I had become very friendly with Greg Norman after playing with him in a pro-am at Adelaide in 1986, and planned to play in the Open

in 1987. The accident put paid to that, but in 1988 I achieved that ambition. It was an incredible experience and, once I'd played a few holes, I thoroughly enjoyed it. Standing on that first tee, though, I was more nervous than I've ever been in a Grand Prix car.

The first day went pretty well, though, and I managed a birdie at the 410-yard par four 18th. I went for a big drive and almost overcooked it. I was in the rough on the left, but it was sitting up reasonably well. I took an eight iron, watched it drop on the green and then heard this great roar from the crowd. My ball was about nine inches from the hole.

I got an unbelievable reception as I walked up that last fairway to the green. When you are in a Grand Prix car you are aware of the crowd and the cheering, but it is just a sea of faces and one noise. On a golf course you can see each and every face, and hear each and every comment. Wags were calling me Nigel Norman and such like. It was a tremendously moving experience, comparable with almost anything I've known in motor racing.

I sank that short putt for a 77, which was just five over par and only two shots off Ian Woosnam's score. Things didn't go so well the second day. I shot an 86 and missed the cut. But that certainly didn't spoil it for me, and I'd love to do it again. I hope I can get in one or two more tournaments.

But to do it well you need practice, practice, practice. You have to dedicate yourself to the game. I am in no position to do that because motor racing still takes priority. Now I am concerned first and foremost with Ferrari. If I can be a winner in Australia in 1989 it will be in the red car No. 27.

*1986 title showdown
. . . so far so good*

*. . . until a tyre and a
dream are shredded*

Lap of Adelaide

Coming out of Foster's Hairpin you've gone up through the gears from second to sixth by the time you cross the start/finish line. Soon, though, you are having to brake fairly hard, down to third or fourth, depending on your gear ratios, for the chicane into Wakefield Road. It's a quick chicane, though. It's just a little flick left and right.

Change up to fifth for the short straight on Wakefield Road before braking hard for the right-hand, ninety-degree corner into Flinders Street. You're down to third gear for this corner. It's quite sharp and also very slippery, so you need to take a little extra care here.

Accelerating out of the corner, up into fourth, for the short stretch of Flinders Street before braking and changing back down to third for another ninety-degree turn. This time it's a left-hander, but again it's tight, it's slippery. It's so easy to go off the road at these corners, especially if your brakes aren't too clever.

Another short burst out of the left-hander before the third of these

consecutive ninety-degree turns. This one is a right-hander and, like the previous two corners, you take it in third. They are all about 70 to 80 m.p.h. corners and can all be tricky if you haven't enough grip and don't have the means of slowing down!

Out of the right-hander, it's up to fourth and down the short straight to East Terrace. You have a quick flick left, then flick right, taking this part in fourth gear. You are coming out sliding, but barely have enough road or time to straighten up because you are suddenly braking hard again for yet another ninety-degree, third-gear right-hander.

This brings you onto Jones Straight, otherwise known around these

Cheers. . . the 1987 toast is Berger . . .

parts as Rundle Road. It is not a particularly long straight, but you can still manage to get up to top gear. So you are accelerating, third to fourth, to fifth, to sixth gear. Then it's back down to fifth just before a right kink.

Through here, you are onto the main straight, which is Dequette-ville Terrace or Brabham Straight. You are obviously soon into sixth gear here, and then it's flat out. It is very, very quick. You are talking about a genuine 190 to 200 m.p.h. and that, of course, is not the kind of speed you normally associate with street circuits.

When my tyre blew in 1986 I was well onto the straight and had to concentrate on keeping it out of the wall. The car was trying to jerk

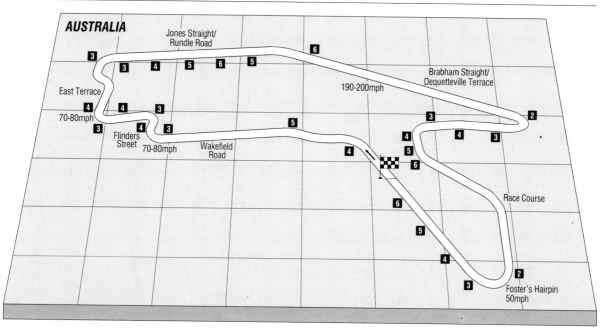

Left: . . . and in 1988 it's Prost

away from me, and it was all I could do to keep pulling it back. At the end of the straight is a right-hander, but by then I had it safely under control. The car rolled into the run-off area and quite gently bumped into the wall. What might have happened doesn't bear thinking about.

Barring mishaps, then, you have used your available horsepower to the full down that long straight and arrived at the braking area for the right-hander. You have to brake very hard, too, because it's a tight turn, the road almost coming back on itself. Down to second gear for this one. Up to third and to fourth for a short stretch with a little left kink in it, to another ninety-degree left. Once more, third gear, very slippery and good brakes a must!

Out of the left-hander, you are changing up to fourth and to fifth, through a quick flick left, heading for Foster's Hairpin. Going into this right-hander, the final corner of the circuit, you are changing down to second gear. It is very, very tight. You are doing about 50 m.p.h. Turning onto the start/finish straight again, you're going up through the gears, second, third, fourth, fifth and sixth, to cross the line and complete the lap.

Adelaide   Fact file

Circuit length: 2·348 miles, 3·778 km.
Race distance: 82 laps (192·536 miles, 309·796 km.)
Qualifying lap record: Gerhard Berger (Ferrari) 1m. 17·267s., in 1987
Race lap record: Gerhard Berger (Ferrari) 1m. 20·416s., at 105·120 m.p.h., in 1987.

Winners: 1985, Keke Rosberg (Williams Honda);1986, Alain Prost (McLaren TAG); 1987, Gerhard Berger (Ferrari); 1988, Alain Prost (McLaren Honda)

Nigel Mansell: 1985, retired (Williams Honda); 1986, retired (Williams Honda); 1987, did not enter (Williams Honda); 1988, accident (Williams Judd)

17 BRANDS AND BEYOND

Circuit: **Brands Hatch**

There is no shortage of takers for Grand Prix motor racing. Nations and circuits all around the globe clamour for the prestige and commercial potential of a date on the Formula One World Championship calendar. What's more, the demand is increasing. Competition is fierce, the lobbying relentless.

For every track welcomed to the fold, another is shown the door. The ever more stringent requirements of FISA and the one-country, one-circuit policy have shut out some famous and infamous venues in recent years. In the United States, Long Beach, Watkins Glen, Dallas and Detroit have gone. Kyalami, in South Africa, was last used in 1985. In Europe, Dijon (France), Zolder (Belgium), Zandvoort (Holland), the new Nürburgring (Germany), and the Osterreichring (Austria) have found themselves out of favour.

Some are unlikely to return, but most dream they will. To that end they are feverishly busy, improving facilities, altering tracks or even rebuilding them completely. And always, of course, they are playing politics. If the end product is a Grand Prix, the means will have been totally justified.

To the hopeful add Brands Hatch, not merely a scintillating car racing track but one of the great arenas of the sporting world. For the drivers it represents a merciless test of skill and nerve, for the public a natural amphitheatre where they can both see and breathe the drama. The spectacle is beguiling, the atmosphere intoxicating.

Brands, alas, became a victim of FISA's decision to end the alternating of venues within a country. The Kent circuit had, since 1964, shared the British Grand Prix with Silverstone. Each was respected in its own right, each was magnificently organized and each thoroughly well supported. But after 1986 Brands was sent into exile. Silverstone had secured an exclusive five-year contract for the race.

It was a devastating blow for the circuit that had developed from a humble grass track in the 1930s to become the busiest motor racing scene in the land. Cyclists and grass track enthusiasts discovered the huge bowl in the Kent countryside to be an ideal location for their pursuits. Spectators were equally appreciative. After the War, cinders were laid on the distinctive kidney-shaped track of the Brands Hatch Stadium.

In 1950, however, a new era dawned over the bowl. The management were persuaded to build a future around car and motorcycle racing, and the then princely sum of £17,000 was invested in a tarmac surface. Britain had its first post-war purpose-built circuit. Among the first drivers to try it out was an ambitious 20-year-old called Stirling Moss. The first victory went to Don Parker, a London garage owner.

Zandvoort . . . trips to the seaside ended in 1985

The Brands rage in the early 1950s was 500cc Formula Three racing. The track itself was originally only one mile long, but extended to 1·24 miles with the introduction of Druids Hill Bend in 1954. That layout became known as the Club Circuit when the Grand Prix extension – a trek out into the woods – was opened in 1960.

The new circuit, more than doubled in length, was to stage some heroic contests. Brands Hatch took over from Aintree as co-hosts of the British Grand Prix and for more than two decades the honours and the spoils were shared with Silverstone. Brands also enjoyed the bonus of European Grands Prix in 1983 and 1985.

First Grand Prix winner at the circuit was, almost inevitably, Jim Clark, who, in his Lotus Climax, was well-nigh unstoppable on home ground. It wasn't until 1985, however, that Britain was celebrating another Brands winner.

For the second time in three years the Grand Prix of Europe was held on this capricious, undulating road and Nigel Mansell enthralled the gallery with his first Formula One success. Not content with that, he followed it up by beating Nelson Piquet in a heart-stopping duel, in the 1986 British Grand Prix, establishing on the way a lap record of 1 minute 9·593 seconds, at a staggering speed of 135·220 m.p.h., witnessed by a crowd of 115,000.

Fate gave Mansell a second chance that day. His driveshaft went seconds after the start, but a pile-up – in which Frenchman Jacques Laffite was injured – forced a re-start. He took over the spare Williams, which had been set up by Piquet, and demonstrated his appreciation in the best possible way.

Jim Clark and his Lotus Climax find the going good, Aintree, 1962

I think it's sad when any established Grand Prix circuit is dropped from the World Championship. Some of the tracks that have gone in recent years are steeped in history. They have played their own particular parts in the story of motor racing. Some, of course, have been particularly important to me in my career.

My very first Grand Prix, in 1980, was at the Osterreichring in Austria. It was a painful debut, too. I sat in a pool of petrol because of a spillage and was burnt in some very delicate places. I have to admit I wasn't too unhappy when my engine went and I had to retire.

But I have fond memories of the Osterreichring as well. It is a spectacular, superfast circuit in beautiful countryside and just happened to be the place where I raced my hundredth Grand Prix, in 1987. I capped the day by winning. Things hadn't gone so well for the circuit that weekend, though. Stefan Johansson ran into a stray deer and was lucky he had no more than shock. The race itself got away at the third attempt after accidents at the first two starts. All of which was held against the organizers when the 1988 calendar was worked out and the Osterreichring lost its place.

We haven't been to Kyalami since I won there in 1985. That was my second win, coming straight after the Grand Prix of Europe at

Kyalami . . . the last race in South Africa, 1985, was won by Mansell

Brands. I also won the last race at Brands, in 1986. It is very satisfying to have won the last race on these three circuits, but hopefully it's not the last we've seen of them.

Brands naturally holds a very special place in my affection. That win in 1985 was the breakthrough I needed. I knew I could win races, but that's not enough. You have to *do* it. To win again the following summer, in those circumstances, was quite incredible.

One way of getting Brands back on the calendar would be to allow Britain a second Grand Prix. Donington or Birmingham might well say they should, in that case, be allowed a chance and I'm certainly not going to argue on that score. All I want to say is that we have some great circuits in England and I'd be happy for more of them to get a look in.

Italy has, in reality, a second Grand Prix in the San Marino race and Monaco is, in effect, a second French race. Britain puts on a great Grand Prix and we have the crowds to support another race. We could then have a rota system to give our various circuits a share. I certainly don't think one circuit should be guaranteed the race for more than, say, three years.

Brands Hatch is a specialist circuit. If you don't know it well there's no way you will go very quickly. It has some strange corners and no matter how you set up the car you won't get it to handle as you wish it to. It's fast, it has sweeping corners, it's up and down. It's interesting, but it can be daunting and hairy. I broke my neck here in my early days, and there have been a few other nasty accidents over the years. It's not a track to take lightly. You are working all the time and you need your wits about you constantly. There's no chance to relax.

Previous page: Osterreichring . . . another track bows out with a Mansell victory, 1987

Lap of Brands Hatch

Past the start/finish line it's quick. You can be doing anything up to 190 m.p.h. in sixth as you approach Paddock Hill Bend. You change down to fourth gear for Paddock, a very tricky right-hander; over a rise and then down into a dip. You have to be very careful not to go too wide out onto the ripple strips. You get negative G, positive G, lateral G. Tricky, yes, but exhilarating, too. You're doing 160 to 170 m.p.h.

You get the positive G in the dip and change to fifth before going up the hill towards Druids. Flat in fifth, staying on the outside. Then you're braking fairly hard and changing down to second gear, pulling across the apex on the inside of the corner. It's slow, about 80 m.p.h.

Out of Druids you're up through the gears, second to third, to fourth, to fifth, and back down the hill. All quick changes before you hit Graham Hill Bend, taking the left-hander flat out. The G-loading here is quite something, and you have to get the corner exactly right.

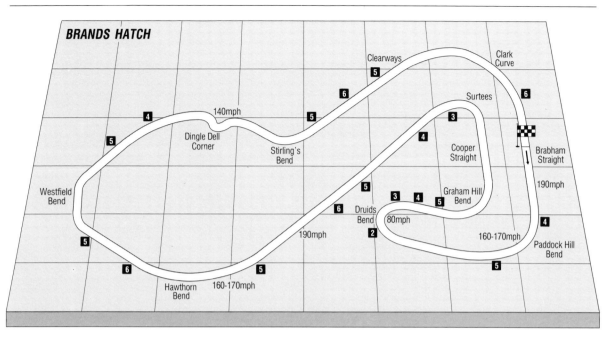

BRANDS HATCH

Clearways

Clark Curve

Surtees

140mph

Dingle Dell Corner

Stirling's Bend

Cooper Straight

Brabham Straight

190mph

Westfield Bend

Graham Hill Bend

Druids Bend

80mph

190mph

160-170mph

Paddock Hill Bend

Hawthorn Bend

160-170mph

You must get tucked in at the apex and you must be very careful not to drift too wide.

Keeping it flat out along the short Cooper Straight to another left-hander at Surtees. It's third or fourth gear out of here as you climb again and go over the brow. It was at this spot where I effectively won the 1986 Grand Prix. Nelson missed a gear change coming out of the bend, and allowed me the opportunity to overtake him into the main straight before Hawthorn Bend. It was such a tight race I knew one little error could be decisive. That was it.

Hawthorn Bend is incredibly fast. You approach it in sixth at 190 m.p.h. and just dab the brakes, changing down to fifth. You go through at 160 to 170 m.p.h. Essential here to keep the car stable. Out of Hawthorn it's a short straight to Westfield Bend, another right-hander. If you've changed up to sixth you're soon back down to fifth again for the bend, which has been altered since 1986. The corner has been chopped off to give you a double apex. It was always a very dangerous corner. You had to be right on the inside, because if you missed the apex you were likely to fall off the circuit on the outside.

Exit Westfield at about 140 m.p.h. and accelerate up to fifth as you head down Dingle Dell. This corner has also been changed. The right-hander now has a chicane in it. Probably fourth gear, as is Stirling's, the left-hander that quickly follows. Here you're keeping the car into the apex on the inside. You have positive camber, which means the car can go round the corner quicker than it could on flat track.

Accelerating out of here, taking care not to get onto the ripple strips because if you do you lose adhesion. Up to fifth and to sixth, then cracking it down to fifth again into Clearways and Clark Curve, the final right-hander. You have to contend with a bit of understeer as the car goes a little light, then a bit of oversteer. Sweeping onto the straight, back into sixth gear and flat out down past the pits and across the start/finish line.

Brands Hatch   Fact file

Circuit length: 2·6002 miles, 4·19 km. (Up to 1986: 2·6136 miles, 4·206 km.)
Race distance: (1986): 75 laps (196·050 miles, 315·511 km.)
Qualifying lap record: Nelson Piquet (Williams Honda) 1m. 6·961s. in 1986
Race lap record: Nigel Mansell (Williams Honda) 1m. 9·593s. at 135·22 m.p.h., in 1986

Winners: (British Grand Prix unless stated): 1964, Jim Clark (Lotus Climax); 1966, Jack Brabham (Brabham Repco); 1968, Jo Siffert (Lotus Ford); 1970, Jochen Rindt (Lotus Ford); 1972, Emerson Fittipaldi (Lotus Ford); 1974, Jody Scheckter (Tyrrell Ford); 1976, Niki Lauda (Ferrari); 1978, Carlos Reutemann (Ferrari); 1980, Alan Jones (Williams Ford); 1982, Niki Lauda (McLaren Ford); 1983 Grand Prix of Europe, Nelson Piquet (Brabham BMW); 1984, Niki Lauda (McLaren TAG); 1985 Grand Prix of Europe, Nigel Mansell (Williams Honda); 1986, Nigel Mansell (Williams Honda)

Nigel Mansell: (British Grand Prix unless stated): 1982, retired (Lotus Ford); 1983 Grand Prix of Europe, 3rd (Lotus Renault); 1984, retired (Lotus Renault); 1985 Grand Prix of Europe, 1st (Williams Honda); 1986, 1st (Williams Honda)

One of the fascinating aspects of Formula One is the way we keep finding new frontiers – and that is the way it should be. As the title says, it's the World Championship. There is still so much more potential for the sport, so many more exciting places to go to. It is a measure of the stature of Formula One that more and more countries are wanting to hold a Grand Prix.

The Russians appear to be serious about staging a race. Hungary took Formula One into Eastern Europe, and it seems there are up to half a dozen possible sites being considered in the USSR. There is talk of interest in China and India, and there has certainly been a lot of behind-the-scenes activity in Singapore. Back in Western Europe we have Barcelona working hard on a new circuit and, of course, the likes of Brands Hatch, Osterreichring and Zandvoort have been making changes and improvements.

One of the rebuilt circuits that hasn't been able to get back a regular place is the Nürburgring. The old Nürburgring was one of the most famous and daunting in the sport. You couldn't possibly race on it with the present cars and the cornering speeds they are capable of. The other problem was that the circuit was so long – more than fourteen miles. It would be virtually impossible adequately to marshal and equip a circuit like that in accordance with current safety requirements.

I've heard people say the new Nürburgring is boring, that the emphasis on safety has taken all the challenge out of it, that it in no way compares with the atmosphere of the original circuit. I think a lot of the criticism is unfounded. If it wasn't for the fact that the circuit stands in the shadows of the old Nürburgring, it would be generally accepted as a good and interesting one.

What makes a good and interesting circuit is a matter of opinion. I think we have yet to see the ideal circuit. Generally the present circuits fall into definite categories. You get those with slow-or medium-speed corners, and you get those with mainly fast corners. If I designed a circuit I'd try to balance the corners; I'd incorporate some of the best fast and slow corners in the world.

I would take the Lesmos from Monza. They are a test for any driver. The Bosch-kurve, at the Osterreichring, is another great challenge, a sweeping right-hand loop taken at upwards of 160 m.p.h. Paddock Hill Bend at Brands Hatch is a fantastic corner. Club and Stowe, at Silverstone, give you a real kick. So fast, so exciting.

With these I would mix some slow corners. The Station Hairpin at Monaco, for instance, is a very special corner. You can't go quickly down there. You struggle round, with the car on full lock, and it's a big effort all the way. A corner doesn't necessarily have to be fast to be challenging, and the Station Hairpin proves the point.

Between these various corners I'd have suitable straights, perhaps where you could actually have a bit of a rest. Then you would be into a complex of corners where you would really need to be on the ball to get the job done properly. The combination and variety of features is essential.

The idea is to examine every aspect of the driver's armoury. You wouldn't have the type of circuit that suits any particular driver. It would be exciting and demanding for all of them. To create such a circuit would be some achievement. For a driver to produce a good lap on such a circuit would also be some achievement and a cause for genuine satisfaction.

Nigel Mansell gets the measure of Brands Hatch for his first Grand Prix win in 1985

Index – ref

Page numbers in *italic* refer to the illustrations

Photograph acknowledgements

The authors and publishers are grateful to the following
for permission to reproduce photographs:

AllSport, pages 53 (top), 57, 102, 156 (top); All Sport/
Michael King, pages 97, 109, 170; AllSport/Mike
Powell, page 35 (bottom); AllSport/Oli Tennant, page
42; AllSport/Pascal Rondeau, pages 2, 3, 84, 111;
AllSport/Vandystadt, pages 23 (top), 38, 40, 58, 88
(top), 98, 103, 112, 118, 127, 138

Diana Burnett, page 18

Colorsport/Sipa Sport, pages 19, 23 (top), 34, 69
(top), 70, 71, 100, 116, 121 (top), 140, 151, 166

Hulton Picture Library, page 76

LAT, pages 7, 11, 24 (left and right), 25, 44 (bottom),
46, 47, 53 (bottom), 54, 55, 73, 77 (bottom), 78, 88
(bottom), 105, 106, 114, 115, 117, 118, 131, 133, 141,
142, 143, 145, 149, 163, 165

Mark Newcombe, pages 12, 22, 29, 30, 62, 63, 64,
74, 82 (right), 83, 125, 129, 135

Nigel Snowdon, pages 14, 65, 93, 95, 121 (bottom),
160

Sutton Photographic, pages 9 (bottom), 15, 17, 33,
35 (top), 39, 44, 48, 49, 69 (bottom), 77 (top), 82 (left),
85, 107, 128, 134, 146, 152, 156 (bottom), 158

John Townsend, page 61

Zooom Photographic Ltd, pages 9 (top), 16, 41, 51,
67, 75, 122, 126

The authors and publishers would also like to thank
Harry Clow for providing the paintings of Hockenheim,
Imola, Jerez, Monaco, Silverstone and Spa and Lovell
Johns Limited for the diagrams of the circuits.